To Heaven & Back

The Journey of a
Roman Catholic Priest

Rev. John Michael Tourangeau, O. Praem.
& Travis James Vanden Heuvel

To Heaven and Back
The Journey of a Roman Catholic Priest

Tourangeau, John M.
Vanden Heuvel, Travis J.

Cover design by Travis Vanden Heuvel. Cover photo: *Mora Valley Sunset* by Shirley D. Vigil, personal collection. Used with permission.

ISBN: 978-0692486597

a Peregrino Press book

De Pere, Wisconsin

This book is dedicated to
John's mother, Elizabeth "Liz" Tourangeau,
his friend and colleague, Cari Schartner,
Travis' wife, Jessica,
and his daughter, Faith Elizabeth.

"Your love gives us strength.
We could not have done this without you!"
With our love and His blessings,
JT & TJ

In the Church's funeral liturgies, we pray that at the time of death 'life has changed, not ended'. Still, we mourn the loss of loved ones and cannot help but anxiously consider our own death. Some choose to seek answers from those who have come close to this moment of life's journey, but remain with us on earth. In recent years, more and more individuals continue to share their experience of near-death or even after-death experiences, describing a real and even tangible description of what they have gone through.

One such testimony of a journey 'to heaven and back' is that of Fr. John Tourangeau. Father's testimony is unique not only because of his ministry as a Catholic priest, but in his own life's journey and the significant impact it has had on his prayer life, personal relationships, need for forgiveness, and the call to witness and share the Gospel, the Good News of life. Describing his life following his experience of death, Father explains that "though initially reluctant to return to earth... I now had a greater clarity of mission and the desire to embrace my life more completely, both personally and professionally. I wanted to live now, more than ever!" Father's experience of death turns to an experience and witness to life – life lived abundantly in Christ.

I recommend this book to readers as it presents the opportunity not only to hear the transformational journey of Father Tourangeau's experience which continues to impact his ministry today, but to be able to draw connections and reflect on our own journey of life and mission which inevitably considers the reality of death. Father presents this reality in a way which provides insight about the true purpose and meaning of our earthly life, recognizing our human dependence upon God's unfailing love for us now and at the hour of our death. In reflecting upon Father's own testimony, may we too continue to grow in our relationship with Jesus Christ together on life's journey as disciples of hope.

The Most Reverend David L. Ricken, DD, JCL
Bishop of Green Bay

In Their Own Words...

"To Heaven and Back tells the story of Fr. John Tourangeau's near death experience that took him to the threshold of heaven and back. That episode alone makes this book undeniably memorable. But what makes it important—and a gift for the reader—is that after this life-altering experience Fr. Tourangeau discovers that if he is truly to move from death back to life, he must deal with his own pain and brokenness, with the memories and fears that hold him bound, and with all the things that rob him of hope. In his discovery that he is called to be a "wounded healer," Fr. Tourangeau becomes a trustworthy spiritual companion and guide who reminds us that we find freedom and peace only when we are not afraid to be the person that God's love summons us to be. Most of all, *To Heaven & Back* is a blessing because it is written with the heartfelt conviction that God always calls us to fullness of life."

Dr. Paul J. Wadell
Professor of Theology & Religious Studies

"I thought I knew Fr. JohnTourangeau. I liked and respected him as a fellow priest and a friend. But I was blown away by the depth and transparency in the telling of his story. Fr John begins with an encounter with the living Christ in the context of a near-death experience and in the light of that meeting he tells his story simply, effect tively and powerfully.

Fr John returns to life seeking to discern his purpose and, while the story is full of faith, hope and love, it is not simplistic. He has to negotiate the challenges of ministry and of family and facing his own demons. In doing so John grows in confidence and faith.

The story is told smoothly. It is a deceptively easy read that packs much power. The book is an expansion of the very popular presentations John has been giving to packed houses in the last few years. He clearly has a message people want and need to hear.

I have recommended this book to the students in my spirituality class. I was personally moved by Fr John's story and felt that much of it was addressed to me personally. I suspect other readers will feel the same way."

Fr. John L. Bostwick, O.Praem.
Adjunct Instructor in Religious Studies

"This is a true account of Father John's journey of his life after death experience. The book is very well written and was hard to put down! Once I started reading it I wanted to keep going until the end! What he explains in his book is exactly what I have been sensing for a few years. Father John writes, 'Life, death and eternal life - heaven and earth- form one great mystery of God's infinite goodness to us from the beginning of creation.'"

Jennifer Cretenson
Amazon Reader

"Fortunate enough to listen to this dynamic gift from God speak in a small church in Escanaba, MI. Reading the book served to further inspire me. It is simply written and a quick read and now I am going to read it with a high lighter and page markers, as I felt such spiritual uplifting and affirmation in his words. I am a Methodist Christian and Father Tourangeau is a Catholic Christian yet through his book I felt being a Christian, regardless of church affiliation, was of the utmost importance. Anyone searching for the wonders of God in their life must read it. In fact, everyone should read it! Such a positive message. Thank you for sharing your story."

Cindy A.
Amazon Reader

"By the title, I thought the book might tell the story of man's spiritual journey to become a priest, but that's not what it's about. It's about Father John's near death experience (NDE) and how it has positively affected his life and relationships, here on earth. As I was reading it, I was touched by how it resonated so deeply with me. Like all of us, Father John wrestles with life...this busy, imperfect, challenging daily ride that brings with it human struggle.

Father John's NDE experience reinforces my belief that we must become as Christ himself practicing unconditional love for others. "While the fullness of heaven cannot be fully experienced in our life here on earth," Father John explains, 'we are able to more fully experience God's love for us through our relationships with others. For it is in and through these relationships that we draw closer to Christ and his promise for us.'"

May the reading of this book bring you the peace and joy that it has brought me.

Dee Geurts-Bengtsonon
Amazon Reader

"The title caught my interest, as well as the subject. The book held my interest, as it was not at all as I expected it to be. It was very compelling and took twists and turns that caused me to think about some preconceived ideas about Catholic Priests.The story made me keep reading. I had to find out what happened next, but the ending was a wonderful surprise."

Amazon Reader

CONTENTS

ACKNOWLEDGEMENTS

peregrinos on the journey

"Peace is a gift of God, often hidden from the wise and
the wealthy, and revealed to those who feel empty, inarticulate, and poor."
(Nouwen, 2001, p. 81)

Writing a book is a labor of love. Many heads, hands, and hearts have contributed to the tapestry of this incredibly moving and inspiring story - my story, your story, our story. It is the story of our lives woven into the greatest story of our faith: that Jesus Christ lived, suffered, died, and was raised to new life in the power of the Holy Spirit by the grace of God, the Creator and Source of all life.

The thousands of people who have attended presentations on my near death experience and sojourn to heaven and back have not only encouraged but also insisted that I set pen to paper and fingers to keyboard and write a book. Why? So that others might discover inspiration, courage, and hope on life's journey. Reluctantly having done so, I found the experience of writing to be both overwhelming and life giving, a truly spiritual exercise and experience that has brought me to a new place of trust in God and humanity. In the enduring wisdom of Fr. Henri Nouwen (1972):

> "Who can take away suffering without entering it?" It is an illusion to think that a person can be led out of the desert by someone who has never been there ... when one has the courage to enter where life is experienced as most unique and most private, one touches the soul of the community. ... It does indeed seem that the Christian leader is, first of all, the artist, who can bind together many people by the courageous act of giving expression to his or her own most personal concerns. (pp. 78-79)

I am particularly grateful to Judy Turba, director of the Norbertine Center for Spirituality at St. Norbert Abbey in De Pere, WI, for her insistence that I speak publicly about my experience of heaven, life, relationships, and ministry. I would never have done so without her encouragement and persistent challenge. And, much to my complete and utter amazement, over 6,000 people have attended some thirty plus presentations on heaven between 2012 and 2014. Clearly there is a hunger and desire for spiritual growth and understanding in the lives of people of faith.

A special note of thanks is extended to my confrere Rev. James B. Herring, O. Praem., who after the first presentation on my near death experience, asked: "When are you going to write the book?" I recall how easily I dismissed his question, but he kept asking and later insisting that I write my story, saying "You have to write about your heaven experience, John. It touches people in a profound way and gives them hope. A new ministry is emerging for you. Write the book now."

This book is also made possible with key recommendations, insights, and encouragement from my friend, colleague, and fellow *peregrino*, Travis Vanden Heuvel, who helped me to tell this story.

Peregrino Press (that is, "Pilgrim Press" translated from Spanish to English) was born when a book deal with a major Catholic publishing company did not materialize. Travis suggested that we form our own publishing company to plan, write, print, distribute, and promote this book. Not only am I blessed by a profound friendship with him, his wife Jessica, and their beautiful daughter Faith, I am so fundamentally and profoundly grateful for his unbridled affirmation, encouragement, challenge, and business acumen, an unparalleled combination of gifts and talents, indeed.

Interestingly enough, while feedback from the general public has been overwhelmingly positive and encouraging, relatively little feedback has come from clergy and religious on my "Heaven" presentations and book adventure. Actually, clergy and religious, more often than not, are silent and distant around the discussion of near death experiences and heaven. Exploration of this reality might well form a template for another book. Time will tell. That being said, special mention of Bishop Robert Morneau, Rev. Alfred McBride, O. Praem., and Bishop David Ricken is herein noted, as they have, and continue, to support and encourage me in the development of this healing ministry grounded in the reality and anticipated full experience of heaven, the Kingdom of God.

I am deeply grateful to many family members and fellow peregrinos who continue to accompany me on this most sacred journey and who insist on remaining anonymous. Without their love, support, commitment, and encouragement, both spiritual and temporal, the publication of this book would have been impossible. Moreover, my life without them would be diminished.

It is also important to me that this story be recounted and

reflected upon with attention not only to detail but also with great accuracy and truth telling. Yet I recognize that my remembering and telling of the story may differ from those who have journeyed and continue to walk with me. To that end, I continue with an important reference that talks about verifiable historical facts, personal remembering of events and people, and contextual framework, judgment, or lens through which levels and layers of interpretation are articulated. In essence, there are three ways of not only remembering but also telling and understanding one's life story.

Shannon's (1998) "A Note to the Reader" in Thomas Merton's book *The Seven Storey Mountain* recommends several different perspectives or contexts in and through which to understand Merton's spiritual autobiography: historical, remembered, and monastic judgment levels.

> First, there is the historical level: what actually happened in his life. Second, there is the remembered level: what Merton was able to recall of the events of his life. Memory is selective, which means that the remembered past may not always coincide with the historical past. Finally, there is the level of monastic judgment. By this I mean that Merton

wrote ... as a monk. His monastic commitment colors the way Thomas Merton ... tells
the story. (pp. xxii-xxiii)

This template of understanding and interpretation of a
story told is most helpful and à propos in the telling of my
journey to heaven and back. Certainly, you, the reader, will be
provided significant historical facts and dates, as well as particular memories of key personal, interpersonal, and spiritual experiences and insights that may or may not harmonize exactly
with historical facts. Additionally, in all aspects, the telling of
my story is filtered through the prism of my lived experience as
both a Religious Order and Diocesan priest.

Finally, I want to express sincere gratitude to one I did
not know in this life, but with whom I feel deeply united in
spirit on the journey through this life into the fullness of eternal
life: Henri Nouwen (1932-1996). In his book *Finding My Way
Home*, Nouwen (2001), a Roman Catholic priest and prolific
spiritual searcher, journeyer, and writer, talks about the need
each of us to find our way home; and, in so doing, to recognize
that "[o]ne of the most radical demands ... is the discovery of
our lives as a series of movements or passages." (p. 133)

Nouwen often spoke of his mission as the lifelong process of reconciling his major depression with his faith, a deci-
sively transformative choice for life that led him to the heart of

the Paschal mystery of Jesus Christ, and one that provided and demonstrated a powerful and faith-filled template for others to do the same, for throughout life, he says... there are choices to be made.

> You choose to live your losses as passages to anger, blame, hatred, depression, and resentment, or you choose to let these losses be passages to something new, something wider, and deeper. The question is not how to avoid loss and make it not happen, but how to choose it as a passage, as an exodus to greater life and freedom. (p. 135)

Indeed, as people of faith we desire greater life and freedom in Jesus Christ from the inside out. Let us humbly enter into, then, this sacred pilgrimage, this journey of faith, friendship, and discipleship. Pray with me for the grace and humility to trust the journey as we embark, because along the way, and for sure in the end, it will lead us into the fullness of God's grace. And, as we walk upon the sacred ground of our lives, let's not be surprised if we discover our deepest selves; that is, the strength and transformative power of our inner voices, as well as the absolutely unconditional gift of peace and wholeness from God who is love and light. Let us help each other remember that our "playing small does not serve the world."

Rev. John Michael Tourangeau, O. Praem.

Fellow Peregrino

Reflection: Fr. Henri Nouwen on mission

Over time, Fr. Nouwen (1932-1996) became convinced that his life work was the reconciliation of his ongoing experience of major depression, his humanity, and his Christian faith. He learned that personal vulnerability was the centerpiece of his search for reconciliation and meaning in Jesus Christ. Moreover, he actively sought out opportunities to share the stories of his life and faith with those in need of healing and hope. He gave witness to his transformative experience of Christian suffering with deeply personal stories grounded in humility, honesty, authenticity, integrity, and love. In the words of Nouwen himself:

> Who can take away suffering without entering it? It is an illusion to think that a person can be led out of the desert by someone who has never been there ... When one has the courage to enter where life is experienced as most unique and most private, one touches the soul of the community. The Christian leader is, first of all, the artist, who can bind together many people by the courageous act of giving expression to his or her own personal concerns. (Nouwen, *The Wounded Healer*, 1972, pp. 78-79)

What needs reconciliation in your life?

_____

_____

_____

_____

_____

_____

_____

_____

_____

_____

_____

_____

_____

_____

_____

_____

_____

_____

_____

In what way(s) might you actively seek out opportunities to share stories of your life and faith?

_____

_____

_____

_____

_____

_____

_____

_____

_____

_____

_____

_____

_____

_____

_____

_____

_____

_____

_____

What is your understanding of the meaning of suffering in a Christian context? How do/can you "enter into" your daily suffering and give it meaning?

_____

_____

_____

_____

_____

_____

_____

_____

_____

_____

_____

_____

_____

_____

_____

_____

_____

_____

"You choose to live your losses as passages to anger, blame, hatred, depression, and resentment, or you choose to let these losses be passages to something new, something wider, and deeper. The question is not how to avoid loss and make it not happen, but how to choose it as a passage, as an exodus to greater life and freedom." (Nouwen, *Finding My Way Home*, 2001, p. 135)

What are the significant losses of your life?

_____

_____

_____

_____

_____

_____

_____

_____

_____

_____

_____

_____

_____

_____

_____

Where in your life do anger, blame, hatred, depression, and resentment dominate/control your thoughts and actions?

_____

_____

_____

_____

_____

_____

_____

_____

_____

_____

_____

_____

_____

_____

_____

_____

_____

_____

_____

_____

_____

How might you tell the stories of faith, family, and friendship as "something new, something wider, and deeper?" Specifically, how have your losses been transformed into stories of hope, healing, reconciliation, and new life?

_____

_____

_____

_____

_____

_____

_____

_____

_____

_____

_____

_____

_____

_____

_____

_____

_____

_____

_____

_____

In what ways have your losses NOT *yet* been transformed into stories of hope, healing, reconciliation, and new life? Specifically, have you ever thought about the losses - the suffering - of your life as an exodus? Could your loss and suffering be a passage to life and freedom?

_____

_____

_____

_____

_____

_____

_____

_____

_____

_____

_____

_____

_____

_____

_____

_____

_____

_____

_____

_____

FORWARD
shine on

"Happiness, not in another place but this place...
Not for another hour, but this hour."
(Walt Whitman)

In a single moment, our lives can be dramatically changed forever. In the middle of a chaotic delivery room, we hear the doctor announce, "It's a boy!" In the foyer, looking through our screen door at the police officer on the front porch, we try to make sense of the words, "There was an accident. I'm sorry. She didn't make it." Standing face-to-face and hand-in-hand, we promise one another, "...for better or for worse, in sickness and in health..." We come together at table with friends and family, "The body of Christ," he says. "Amen," we reply. In a single moment, our lives can be dramatically changed forever.

To Heaven & Back: The Journey of a Roman Catholic Priest is a story about moments; moments that have the power to dramatically change our lives forever. This is a story about the moments leading up to, during, and following the severe heart attack of a Catholic priest. More than that, though, this is a story that inspires each and every one of us to make moments of our own. As we journey with Fr. John through the ups and downs of his life, we are encouraged to reflect upon the moments when we have felt loved, betrayed, exhausted, depressed, hopeful, or at peace.

In the pages to come, you'll hear about John's trip to heaven and back, the conversation he had with Jesus, his reconciliation with his father, and the affection he has for his fellow pilgrims on life's journey. Subtle in some places, not so subtle in others, John challenges us to create moments in our own lives where we can journey, converse, forgive, and love with those around us. He calls us to pay particularly close attention to those who are on the margins – the poor, the lonely, the forgotten – that we might be Christ to and for one another.

Answering the question "WWJD?" (What Would Jesus Do?) isn't always easy. St. John reminds us in his Gospel that God is love (4:16). This story speaks to the very heart of that love; a love that is tangible and everlasting. If we can recognize goodness and love in our personal relationships, in our work, in our communities, then we can begin to know and delight in the presence of God in our lives.

When given the opportunity to help John tell and share his story, I jumped in with both feet. And while his personal *story* is interesting, it is his personal *mission* that really resonates with me. When you read John's writings, hear him preach at Mass, listen to him give a presentation, or converse with him over coffee, his passion is infectious. He ministers in a way that calls others to action; leaving many people to think "I want to journey with him!"

Part of the attraction to John comes from his humanity. We sometimes forget that priests put their pants on the same way the rest of us do. John goes out of his way to remind us that he is – no different than you or I – "just another child of Christ on his way home." John speaks of his own sins and failures, making this story that much more relevant and relatable. Because of his example, we are better able to explore the darkness and brokenness in our own lives. In Marianne Williamson's words, "as we let our own light shine, we unconsciously give other people permission to do the same. As we are liberated from our own fear, our presence automatically liberates others." In this book, John invites all of us to let our lights shine.

Shine on.

Travis James Vanden Heuvel
President & Publisher
Peregrino Press
www.peregrino.press

Reflection: The paradox and gift of "fear"

"Our deepest fear is not that we are inadequate. Our deepest fear is that we are powerful beyond measure. It is our light, not our darkness that most frightens us . . . You are a child of God. Your playing small does not serve the world. There is nothing enlightened about shrinking so that other people won't feel insecure around you. We are all meant to shine, as children do. We were born to make manifest the glory of God that is within us. It's not just in some of us; it's in everyone. And as we let our own light shine, we unconsciously give other people permission to do the same. As we are liberated from our own fear, our presence automatically liberates others." (Williamson, *A Return to Love: Reflections on the Principles of "A Course in Miracles"*)

What is your deepest fear?

_____

_____

_____

_____

_____

_____

_____

Do you believe - really believe - that you are beloved of God
… that you are God's child?

_____

_____

_____

_____

_____

_____

_____

_____

_____

_____

_____

_____

_____

_____

_____

_____

_____

_____

_____

In what ways do you "play it small" in the world and in relationship with others?

_____

_____

_____

_____

_____

_____

_____

_____

_____

_____

_____

_____

_____

_____

_____

_____

_____

_____

_____

_____

_____

_____

In what ways do you desire "to let you light shine?"

_____

_____

_____

_____

_____

_____

_____

_____

_____

_____

_____

_____

_____

_____

_____

_____

_____

_____

PROLOGUE
the lonely, broken hearted, and battle scarred

"When you're standing on the edge of nowhere there's only one way up.
So your heart's got to go there through the darkest nights ... This is a song
for the lonely ... for the broken hearted, battle scarred ... Can you hear this
prayer? 'Cause someone's there for you."
(Cher, Live: The Farewell Tour, 2003)

I often jest that I feel much like the musical artist Cher, in that the presentations about my near death and heaven experience are much like her farewell tour, a tour that never seemed to come to an end. The public wanted more, and, indeed, she gave her all with marked enthusiasm. I try to do the same.

The combination of powerful words written by Barry,

Taylor, and Torch (2014), coupled with Cher's vocal gift and uncompromising human spirit and positive attitude, opened the door to a profound reality: hope. This reality of hope lifted people who felt entombed in the darkest of nights - alone, broken hearted, and battle scarred - so that they might sing forth in joy, freedom, and peace, ultimately knowing they do not journey alone in life.

In much the same manner, Nouwen (1972) says, "The first and most basic task of contemporary Christian leaders is to lead people out of the land of confusion into the land of hope." But one cannot lead, guide, or show the way of hope to others if she or he has not entered into the depths of the self; unless, in other words, they find "the courage to be explorers of the new territory within themselves and to articulate their discoveries …" (p. 44)

Courage to make a personal choice to explore the inner domain of the self is one thing. Encountering and sustaining a trusted companion and guide with whom to explore is much more challenging and demanding. Quite frankly, this cooperative exploration has been my challenge over the years. Finding and sustaining a spiritual companion continues to be difficult, indeed, if not nearly impossible. Goodness of fit—specifically a spirituality of wisdom and love grounded in hope born of dark nights and broken hearts—has been hard to come by in a spiritual companion, in a mentor, guide, and director. I take heart, however, in the fact that great spiritual men and women throughout history were challenged in much the same manner as they struggled to find wise and discerning spiritual company.

> The greatest complaint of the Spanish mystics St. Theresa of Avila and St. John of the Cross, was that they lacked a spiritual guide to lead them along the right paths and enable them to distinguish between creative and destructive spirits. (p. 41)

In my teaching and preaching ministry on near death and heaven, I have come to know beyond a shadow of doubt that people want to explore the interior life, but don't always know how or where to begin. People desire healing and transformation from the inside out, but often wander aimlessly. They constantly are on the lookout for spiritual guides and companions to gently and lovingly chart the course and accompany them to new life in the Spirit. A woman who attended one of my heaven presentations told me (rather prophetically):

> Fr. John, you don't need any more academic degrees. You're doing your homework and you are a profound example of hope. Your honesty

is refreshing and your faith is evident. Don't look any farther for your mission in life; telling your story is clearly your mission and ministry now. For this you came back from heaven. You are a gift to us. What don't you understand? You are called to be a spiritual guide.

Shannon (1998), founding president of the Thomas Merton Society, sheds some important light on the spiritual work of searching and sharing the stories of our lives. Specifically, he refers to Fr. Thomas Merton's The *Seven Storey Mountain* as "a twentieth-century 'version' of *The Confessions of St. Augustine* ... an autobiography with a pattern and meaning valid for all of us," and that "we can identify with his searching," because "[h]is story contains perennial elements of our common human experience. That is what makes it profoundly universal" (pp. xix-xxi). Indeed, I'm in outstanding company with St. Augustine and Thomas Merton as great companions on the journey! Both serve as spiritual guides and mentors.

I never entertained thoughts about publicly speaking about my near death and heaven experience, fearing most, I suppose, that I would not be believed. But with some coaxing, encouragement, and dogged determination of those close to me, I began presenting and teaching some three years ago. The first presentation was on February 28, 2012, a rather cold and crisp winter evening in Northeastern Wisconsin. Some 150 people attended that first presentation, and many asked when I would be presenting again. I realized that evening that I needed to pray for God's grace, as well as for a willingness and openness to be God's instrument of healing and peace.

This ministry, of course, is shaped by my experience of life and faith, beginning with my family of origin. I am the eldest of four children – three boys and a girl – born to Roger and Elizabeth (Kutches) Tourangeau, Sr., on March 4, 1958, in Escanaba, MI, at St. Francis Hospital. Immigrant grandparents from French-speaking Canada and Croatia (formerly Yugoslavia) settled in the Upper Peninsula of Michigan years earlier to create a new life full of opportunity grounded in deep faith, culture, and the land.

I left home at the age of fifteen to attend a boarding high school where young men are educated and prepared for Christian leadership and service. In all honesty, my motivation for leaving home was mixed and complex. Of course there was the reality of deep generational faith and Roman Catholic practice; and, there was also the painful, and sometimes embarrassing, realities of mom's lifelong challenges with depression and dad's struggle with alcoholism. Family dynamics were often uncertain - that is, quite unpredictable - given the challenges depression and alcoholism fueled among us.

It was at St. Lawrence Seminary, Mt. Calvary, WI,

where I began to contemplate Religious Order life and priesthood, as well as to discover my love and aptitude for all things academic, though I would not flourish academically until I began post-graduate studies. In addition to my undergraduate degree in Sociology (St. Norbert College, De Pere, WI), I hold several graduate degrees: Master of Divinity (Catholic Theological Union, Chicago, IL), Master of Social Work (Highlands University, Las Vegas, NM), and Master of Business Administration (University of Phoenix, Albuquerque, NM). As of the writing of this book, I am in the dissertation phase of a PhD in Organization Development (Benedictine University, Lisle, IL).

I was ordained as a Roman Catholic priest on June 6, 1986 – the Solemnity of St. Norbert, the founder (1121) of the Religious Order to which I belong – at St. Norbert Abbey, De Pere, WI. I have served both as a priest of St. Norbert Abbey and of the Archdiocese of Santa Fe, NM. Ministry placements have included Lima, Peru (South America), Chicago, IL, Albuquerque, Mora, Clovis, and Taos, NM, and most recently, De Pere, WI, at St. Norbert Abbey and St. Norbert College.

I am a man of deep and abiding faith; I am also a sinful man in need of God's grace, healing, forgiveness, and reconciliation. To build upon Nouwen's (1972) simple, yet dynamic, image, I am becoming a "wounded healer." I am convinced that my mission in life as a man of faith and priest of God is to be a wounded healer:

for all ministers are called to recognize the sufferings of their time in their own hearts, and to make that recognition the starting point of their service …(and)…service will not be perceived as authentic unless it comes from a heart wounded by the suffering about which we speak. (p. 4)

Nouwen continues:

Moreover, becoming a wounded healer is the basis for a spiritual leadership of the future, because only those who are able to articulate their own experiences can offer themselves to others as sources of clarification. Christian leaders are, therefore, first of all those who are willing to put their own articulated faith at the disposal of those who ask for help…they are servant of servants, because they are the first to enter the promised but dangerous land, the first to tell those who are afraid what they themselves have seen, heard, and touched. (pp. 42-43)

The wounded healer is one who does not fear death or life. The wounded healer holds potential to be a powerful and humble "spiritual guide" because she or he can journey with others, to lead them "along the right paths and enable them to distinguish between creative and destructive spirits" (p. 41). The wounded healer never seeks power or prestige, but recognizes that the path to freedom and wholeness is discovered in weakness. Nouwen (2001) offers these words of counsel and wisdom.

> The most insidious, divisive, and wounding power is the power used in the service of God. ... An unfriendly or judgmental word by a minister or priest, a critical remark in church about a certain lifestyle, a refusal to welcome people at the table, an absence during an illness or death, and countless other hurts often remain longer in people's memories than other more world-like rejections. Thousands of separated and divorced men and women, numerous gay and lesbian people, and all of the homeless people who felt unwelcome in the houses of worship of their brothers and sisters in the human family have turned away from God because they experienced the use of power when they expected an expression of love. (p. 28)

In summary, this book is about my near death experience and the subsequent impact of it on my mission, specifically on my life and ministry. It is intended to be an expression of love grounded in Christian hope. It is, in the words of pop singer Cher, a "song for the lonely," a song for those "standing on the edge of nowhere . . . the broken hearted, battle scarred." It is a prayer to be heard, because "someone's there for you . . . someone's there for you . . . it's gonna' be alright . . . through the darkest night . . . you're gonna' see the light."

CHAPTER ONE
bread, wine, and a broken heart

"Lord, you are holy indeed, the fountain of all holiness. Let your Spirit come upon these gifts to make them holy, so that they may become for us the body and blood of our Lord, Jesus Christ."
(Catholic Church & Vatican Council II, 1983, Eucharistic Prayer II)

It was a decisive moment in time, one not easily overlooked, forgotten, or even dismissed. It was 5:40 p.m. on January 16, 1993, and I was in the middle of presiding at the Saturday Mass, the Vigil Mass of the Second Sunday of the year. The Scripture readings that day spoke of being called and chosen for hope and holiness through baptism, not only for repentance and forgiveness of sin, but a baptism that makes Jesus known to all as the Son of God, "the fountain of all holiness." The Catholic Mass - the celebration of the holy Eucharist - has always been important in my life and the life of both my immediate and extended families. As stated in the *Catechism of the Catholic Church* (2012): "The Eucharist is 'the source and summit' of the Christian life" (1324). The Catechism further affirms: "by the Eucharistic celebration we already unite ourselves with the heavenly liturgy and anticipated eternal life, when God will be all in all" (1226) *The United States Catholic Catechism for Adults* (USCCB, 2006) says it this way:

> The ultimate goal of a life of faith is eternal union with God in heaven. Through the gift and experience of faith, we are able not only to look ahead to what awaits us, but also to experience here some of God's divine life, "a taste in advance" of our sharing life with him forever...because...believers know the strength, the wisdom, the confidence and hope that a life of faith gives. (p. 41)

Having just completed the epiclesis - the calling down of the Holy Spirit of God upon the bread and wine upon the altar –

I continued with the prayerful recitation the words of the Institution Narrative of Eucharistic Prayer II, the words of Jesus at the time of the Last Supper, when I suddenly began to feel sick. I first felt nauseous, then a cold and clammy sweat ensued followed by lightheadedness, a tightness in my chest, a pain down my left arm, and a bit of shortness of breath. The thought that I might be having a heart attack crossed my mind, but, of course, I didn't dwell on it. Anyway, how could it be? A man of almost thirty-five years of age could not be experiencing a cardiac event of such magnitude. "It's simply the flu," I concluded, and continued with the words of consecration:

> On the night he was betrayed he took bread …
> "Take this, all of you, and eat it. This is my body,
> which will be given up for you." … When supper
> was ended, he took the cup … and said: "Take
> this, all of you, and drink from it. This is the cup
> of my blood … It will be shed for you … Do this
> in memory of me." (Eucharistic Prayer II)

I finished celebrating Mass and stayed to greet and visit with the gathered community of faith. I remained in church to spend time with the choir in rehearsal thereafter, all the while thinking about what my mom would do for us as kids when one of us was sick with the flu. This provided me a deep sense of comfort and security as I anticipated going home to the rectory for the evening. I would put on my flannel pajamas and lie down on the couch in the living room to watch television with either a bowl of Jell-O or ice cream. Mom's medicine awaited me. I knew that I wasn't feeling well, but no one else seemed to be aware of my apparent dilemma. I guess I was holding it all together pretty well at the time.

And so, having made my way to the rectory, and, donned with pajamas and trashcan in hand (after all, I had the flu), I made myself comfortable on the living room sofa with my bowl of ice cream. I turned on the television, sat down, and enjoyed my ice cream, all the while anticipating a good and long sleep-filled night, with thoughts of waking up in the morning feeling refreshed and in good health.

Much to my surprise and dismay, having only slept for a brief time, perhaps an hour or so, I suddenly awoke with the realization that I was having extreme difficulty breathing. I could barely draw a breath. This got my full and immediate attention, and I said out loud to myself as I was walking to my bedroom to change clothes to go the hospital: "This is a heart attack!"

Prior to changing clothes, I called a young couple that lived close by. Actually, this couple led the choir rehearsal earlier in the evening. "Would you please come to the rectory and drive me to the emergency room? I think I need to see a doctor." "Yes, of course, Father. We'll be right there," came the response. And, I added, "take your time; don't hurry. I need to get dressed."

"Could it be my time to join mom in heaven?" was the question I asked myself as I walked toward the bedroom to change from my pajamas into my clergy suit. Once dressed, I made my way to the front door of the rectory, peering through the window for several minutes until my ride arrived.

The young couple greeted me warmly and expressed concern for how I was feeling. I calmly told them that I had an upset stomach and was experiencing some difficulty breathing. That being said, as we drove to the hospital emergency room, an unarticulated anxious feeling prevailed. Time seemed to stand still as I repeatedly asked myself: "Am I going to die tonight?" I was frightened and scared, but didn't verbalize my feelings to the couple. Impending death was all I could think about at the moment.

"Am I going to die tonight?"

CHAPTER TWO
hopes, dreams, and fears

"Hospitality is the virtue that allows us to break through the
narrowness of our own fears and to open our houses to the stranger…"
(Nouwen, 1972, p. 95)

I believe that I am able to be healing balm and hope for
others on the journey because I continue to learn how to share
in and live more completely and fully the mission and ministry
of Jesus. The essence of faith - of believing and serving others
out of a font of deep trust - is nothing less than sharing intimately in the paschal mystery; that is, in the life, suffering,
death, and resurrection of Jesus. It is the experience of making

sense of lived life and faith personally and with others in community as a prologue to future discipleship in a spirit of radical hospitality.

I believe this story must be told because, as Christians, we are invited to journey with each other. Like Jesus, gathered with his family and friends at the hometown synagogue, reading from the ancient scroll of the prophet Isaiah, we, too, are sent on a mission in humble service of others to proclaim a time acceptable to the Lord.

> He has sent me to proclaim liberty to captives and
> recovery of sight to the blind, to let the oppressed
> go free, and to proclaim a year acceptable to the
> Lord. (Luke 4:18b –19)

I grew up in a devout Roman Catholic family in Escanaba, in the Upper Peninsula of Michigan. My parents met and married in their early twenties. We were a solid middle-class family, with dad working at a local paper mill and mom managing household affairs and caring for her children. Both dad and mom were strong in their faith and active in church worship and outreach. We were a good and decent family, but by no means perfect.

Not only did I grow to love the Church, but I also developed a passion for learning. This love and passion fueled my desire to attend Catholic grade school. Yet, the financial situation of my family at the time made this impossible. In time, dad and mom consented to my desire to attend the local Catholic high school, but unfortunately, due to low enrollment and financial challenges, Holy Name High School was forced to close when I was in the eighth grade. Thus, I continued my education at the local public high school in Escanaba for two years.

By God's good grace, I had the unexpected opportunity to attend St. Lawrence Seminary, a Catholic boarding school in Mt. Calvary, WI, for my last two years of high school. My parents supported my decision to do so, albeit with one significant caveat; I had to pay my own way. Luckily, I had been a paperboy for several years and saved all of my earnings, $1,300 to be exact. Not surprisingly, the total cost of room, board, and tuition was $650 per year. I was on my way to boarding school; it was meant to be.

The two years I spent at St. Lawrence were wonderful, encouraging, and growth-filled. I made lifelong friends, learned about and experienced healthy community life, embraced prayer (both personal and communal, devotional and Eucharistic), and welcomed the experience of rigorous academic study. Along the way, I slowly warmed up to the idea that I might very well have a vocation to religious life and priesthood.

Upon completing my high school studies at St. Lawrence in 1976, I decided to enter the Capuchin Franciscan pre-novitiate program in Brothertown, WI, just a few miles from the high school. As members of this community, we had the option of beginning college studies at one of two local schools: Marian College in Fond du Lac, WI, or Lakeland College near Sheboygan, WI. I chose the latter because the financial aid package was more robust.

After two years of study at Lakeland College, I was encouraged and bolstered by the ongoing spiritual guidance and the holy and loving example of my paternal uncle, Brother Clement Tourangeau, O. Praem., to further explore a religious vocation. I made application to and was accepted into the novitiate of the Norbertine Community at St. Norbert Abbey on August 28, 1978, the Solemnity of St. Augustine whose Rule of Life we Norbertines follow. I was twenty years old. After successful completion of six years of initial formation (including being graduated from St. Norbert College in 1981 and Catholic Theological Union in 1986, Simple Vows in 1981 and 1982, Solemn Vows in 1985, and ordination as a deacon on September 14, 1985), I was ordained as a priest on June 6, 1986, the Solemnity of St. Norbert (the founder of the Norbertine Order in 1121 in France).

I was assigned as a transitional deacon and as a first-year priest to minister at Providence of God Parish, an inner city immigrant Mexican community in the Archdiocese of Chicago. Thereafter, I was transferred to the budding Norbertine mission at Santa María de la Vid Priory in Albuquerque, NM. I served as an associate pastor at Our Lady of the Most Holy Rosary Catholic Community. After two years of ministry there, I decided to begin the process of incardination (i.e., process of membership) into the Archdiocese of Santa Fe as an archdiocesan priest, serving immigrant Mexican and generational New Mexican communities. This transition afforded me the opportunity to serve in rural faith communities throughout the archdiocese, communities with particular pastoral and leadership needs that I could meet given my experience, training, and expertise. Within the vast Archdiocese of Santa Fe, I served as pastor of St. Gertrude the Great and her fifteen missions in Mora, Our Lady of Guadalupe in Clovis with the Mission of San José in Texico, San Francisco de Asís in Ranchos de Taos, and St. Anne's in the South Valley of Albuquerque.

Without doubt, the most challenging assignment of my New Mexican sojourn was as pastor of Our Lady of Guadalupe Parish in Clovis and Mission of San José in Texico. I began my ministry there in the summer of 1991. The Franciscan Friars had served the parish since its founding and had come to the decision that they could no longer meet the pastoral needs given their diminishing personnel resources. As the Franciscans bid farewell to their beloved people, I was making final preparations for my transition to southeastern New Mexico. I was excited, anxious, and full of energy to begin this new assignment.

I arrived at the rectory of Our Lady of Guadalupe the day after the departure of the Franciscan Friars. In retrospect, it was an extremely demanding time of transition with unrealistic expectations on my part, as well as on the part of the community of faith. Quite naturally, the community wanted its beloved Franciscan Friars to return home, while I, in the midst of a community in mourning, convinced myself in my youthful naiveté that I would work harder, and that sooner than later, the community would welcome me and love me as they did the Franciscan Friars. I reasoned that all would be copacetic.

I worked long hours, didn't eat very well, and was smoking more than two packs of cigarettes a day. I wasn't exercising much either. And, not surprisingly, my personal prayer life was on a steep decline as well. Ultimately, this mix of external realities and internal personal dynamics would prove to be a recipe for disaster; a life-altering disaster. I had no idea what awaited me. I convinced myself that I was a good and faithful servant working day and night for the good of the people in the parish and ultimately for the Kingdom of God … God would not let me down.

A year and a half into this pastoral assignment and ministerial experience, great strides were being made and everything looked rather impressive from the outside in. I thought we were doing well as a community of faith and I was feeling successful as a spiritual leader, pastor, and spiritual companion. I was shepherding a sizable and growing community of faith, overseeing the management of ever-increasing temporal assets, and was spearheading a parish office building expansion project. I felt welcomed, accepted, and loved.

CHAPTER THREE
relinquishing control

The drive from the parish rectory to the local hospital emergency room in Clovis, NM, seemed to last an eternity, though it was only a short distance away, perhaps a mile or two, as I recall. The question - "Am I going to die tonight?" - resounded and repeated itself over and over and over in my head.

I declined a wheelchair escort into the emergency room, walking into the reception area where a nurse greeted me, "Father John, what are you doing here? It's late and there's nobody here who needs to see a priest." Her question and comment brought a note of humor to an otherwise very serious situation. "I think I need to see a priest. Call Fr. Mark, please; I think I'm having a heart attack!"

Not surprisingly, the tone in the ER changed dramatically, as if in an instant. Everyone immediately transitioned into crisis mode, so much so that, in what seemed like a few seconds, I was stripped of my clothes and placed on a cold table with a skimpy hospital gown draped over me. There were several nurses and an ER doctor attending to me; and, needless-to-say, I was feeling rather vulnerable and deprived of privacy and personal space. Naked and extremely vulnerable, I wanted my clothes back.

While connecting me up to machines and monitors and placing nitroglycerine tablets under my tongue, the doctor looked at me and said: "You waited too long to get here, sir." I was petrified. There was no immediate response on my part, only a deep sense of fear that completely paralyzed my inner spirit. Much to my surprise, he spoke again: "Sir, you've waited too long to get here. You're not going to make it." He continued: "If you believe in God, this is the time to make peace." In that very moment, I said to myself, "What do you mean, 'If I believe in God?' Of course I believe in God! I'm a man of faith and a Catholic priest!"

I quickly realized that I was not living in what might be perceived as a dress rehearsal any longer; I was in the final act of what seemed like – at least in the moment – a very short life of thirty-four years. "This is it," I thought, "the final act in the performance of my life." I was paralyzed by intense fear. Thereafter, as if in an instant, I experienced a profound epiphany, "If this is really it, I don't have much choice, so why not just let go, trust God, and let God be God?" Miraculously, I relinquished control in that moment and felt my whole body relax. I was calm and there was a profound sense of peace that came over me, followed by a most memorable review of life in a cinema-like production.

It was a complete life review. I don't know how long it lasted, but it was wonderful. It was so wonderful and memorable that I didn't want it to end. There were people and experiences featured that I hadn't thought about for years. Everything about my life was coming back in picture form. And, surprisingly, the first picture - the first movie frame - was of me riding a red tricycle; I was about 3 or 4 years old.

Years later, after telling my dad about this life review experience, he disappeared into the attic of the family home only to emerge and descend with an old black and white photo, saying, "Here's that picture of you on your red tricycle." Coincidence, perhaps, but I really don't think so.

In addition to that powerful initial movie frame of me on a red tricycle, I remember, in general, additional life review highlights that included joyful family holiday gatherings and outings, as well as experiences with siblings and friends. With time, however, many of the details of the life review have faded, but what remains with me to this day is that the life review was filled with happy events and human interactions shrouded in love.

Back in the emergency room with all its drama and activity, as the life review was coming to an end, I heard the doctor say to his colleagues, "We're losing him!" My spirit departed from my body and floated to the upper corner of the emergency room. How odd and how interesting; yet, it was remarkably peaceful and acceptable. I had a deep sense of normalcy. I remember thinking that this is "the way it should be at the end of life on earth." I was "observing" everything unfolding in the emergency room from within the depth of my spirit, my soul having separated from my body. "I think I'm dead," I said to myself. "But am I really dead?"

I could "see" everything and everyone. I observed my body on the emergency room table while at the same time listening to the beeping heart monitor. I also recall hearing the doctor say, "I think we're losing him." Then suddenly, I was no longer in the emergency room, but enveloped in a bright white light. I was acutely aware of, and deeply in tune with, a sense of movement. I was on my way to some undisclosed destination. I thought, "Might I be going to heaven?" Something deep inside of my spirit told me: "Enjoy the journey. Be in the fullness and the completeness of the moment."

Remarkably, I surrendered and entered into the peace at hand. I then realized that others were with me; I was not alone. I had friends with me on my journey. I was surrounded by a community of family and friends that had already made the journey into the fullness of heaven. Jesus was with me, too. What great solace . . . the reign of God at hand . . . the time of fulfillment. "I believe!" . . . "Yes, I do believe in God!"

CHAPTER FOUR
faith, doubt, and suffering

"A faith without some doubts is like a human body without any antibodies in it. People who blithely go through life too busy or indifferent to ask hard questions about why they believe as they do will find themselves defense-less against either the experience of tragedy or the probing questions of a smart skeptic."
(Keller, 2008, p. xvii)

Coming home - coming home to the heart - is what Jesus was and is all about, both literally and figuratively. Not unex-pectedly or unpredictably, then, Jesus' public ministry begins at home after his challenging time of suffering and doubt in the desert as he confronted sin and Satan. While at home, as was his custom, Jesus goes to synagogue with his parents, Mary and Joseph. While in the midst of worship, Jesus is handed the scroll of the Prophet Isaiah, unrolls it and begins to read, proclaiming in part:

> The spirit of the Lord is upon me, because he has anointed me to bring glad tidings to the poor. He has sent me to proclaim liberty to captives and recovery of sight to the blind, to let the oppressed go free, and to proclaim a year acceptable to the Lord. (Luke 4:18-19)

Jesus' proclamation and preaching of the Word are marked by freedom and a sense of release from all that holds *us* bound. In turn, we must support and journey with others in their desire to be released from all that holds *them* bound.

In this context, let's pause for a moment of reflection, calling to mind those things and realities that hold us bound as individuals, families, communities, and nations. What broken relationships, unfulfilled dreams and expectations, addictive patterns and behaviors, jealousy and competition, unfulfilling or inadequate work, physical limitations and chronic conditions, or political unrest and warring might we have? Simply stated, what has a grip on us and takes life away from self and others? What, in our lived experience, challenges our faith and belief in God?

As a result of significant chaos throughout life, I learned to protect myself and be directed primarily by others. I came to be an expert at reading the external cues of others and doing whatever was necessary to accommodate them. This, I believe in large part, came from growing up in a family environment with addiction and mental health issues.

Dad struggled with alcohol and mom with major depression. Dad interacted with brute force, physically, verbally, and emotionally. Mom withdrew, seeking solace in sleep and food. So, as the eldest, I became "parentified" at a young age, carefully managing the external familial environment, while at the same time suppressing any and all personal issues and/or concerns regarding both human and spiritual growth and development.

How interesting, then, that in light of these familial realities, I would have experienced a major cardiac event, a heart attack. My heart had literally broken under the built-up pressures over the years. I believe it was not at all a coincidence, for the body speaks, and speaks definitively, when thoughts, issues, and emotions are repressed over time. Unattended matters of the heart often result in physical, emotional, and spiritual sickness, illness, and/or trauma.

Reflection: Jesus' mission

"The spirit of the Lord is upon me, because he has anointed me to bring glad tidings to the poor. He has sent me to proclaim liberty to captives and recovery of sight to the blind, to let the oppressed go free, and to proclaim a year acceptable to the Lord." (Luke 4:18b-19)

"The Son of Man has come to search out and save what was lost." (Luke 19:10)

In what ways are you broken and struggling?

_____

_____

_____

_____

_____

_____

_____

_____

_____

_____

_____

_____

_____

What holds you captive?

_____

_____

_____

_____

_____

_____

_____

_____

_____

_____

_____

_____

_____

_____

_____

_____

_____

_____

_____

_____

_____

In what ways do you need to be set free?

_____

_____

_____

_____

_____

_____

_____

_____

_____

_____

_____

_____

_____

_____

_____

_____

_____

_____

What relationships in your life need healing?

_____

_____

_____

_____

_____

_____

_____

_____

_____

_____

_____

_____

_____

_____

_____

_____

_____

_____

_____

Is your journey of faith intimately connected with Jesus?

_____

_____

_____

_____

_____

_____

_____

_____

_____

_____

_____

_____

_____

_____

_____

_____

_____

_____

_____

_____

_____

CHAPTER FIVE
to heaven and back

"The Reign of God is already in your midst."
(Luke 17:21b)

How does one begin to share with others - to talk about - a journey to heaven, a conversation with Jesus, and a return to life on earth? One would think that such a life-altering experience would be told and received without reservation and with great enthusiasm. Yet, generally speaking, that is not the reality. Most people resist talking about a near-death experience because of a fundamental apprehension that others will not believe them. Typically, it takes many, many years for one to find the confidence and venue to do so. It took me more than twenty years to tell my own story.

The Reign of God - the fullness of the Kingdom of God - is marked by freedom and a sense of release from all that holds us bound. This lesson and reality became crystal clear as I stood at the threshold of heaven in conversation with Jesus. To this day, I vividly recall telling Jesus how happy I was to be at heaven's threshold and that I couldn't wait to experience the fullness of heaven. Much to my surprise, though, he indicated that I was destined for a return to life on earth, a reality that completely surprised, saddened, and frustrated me. I so desired the deep peace I was experiencing in that moment for all eternity. How could I be denied the fullness of heaven?

In the calming, encouraging, and loving voice of a dear and trusted friend, Jesus spoke: "Your work on earth is not done, John." I had to return to earth because my work on earth was not done? Really? How could it be? So, reluctantly, taking Jesus' lead, I asked: "What is the work that awaits me on earth?" He indicated that, upon my return, I would have the opportunity to discover the answer to that question. I was puzzled and confused. Why couldn't Jesus simply tell me what that work was, so I could complete it in a timely manner and return to heaven? But it wasn't going to be that simple or easy.

Little did I know what awaited me and what would be

asked of me back on earth. Like others before me, I had to regroup and embark upon a serious assessment of my life – my spiritual life in particular – and come to recognize a deeper relationship with myself and others. My journey to heaven and back was a transformative experience that provided a new clarity and understanding. This would serve as the springboard for a deeper and more profound passion for life, love, and relationship with self and others, and for the peace of heaven that begins here on earth.

Suddenly, and without any desire on my part, my spirit – my soul – was in the process of returning to my physical body. I heard the doctor say to the nurses that there was a heartbeat, at which time my soul and body were suddenly reunited. "What am I to do now?" I thought. It was a perplexing and unsettling moment in time for me. I felt alone. I was scared. I wanted my mom, dad, and siblings – my family – at my side to love, comfort, and assure me.

My near-death experience and return to life on earth, including my transformative conversation with Jesus at the threshold of heaven, continues to serve as a springboard for ongoing reflection, prayer, and conversation as a human being, a man of faith, and a Catholic priest. I am called every day to enter more fully the very mystery of faith and presence of God, including tending to the significant relationships in my life as a good steward of all that God has given me. I am not only called to love self and others, but to allow them to love me in return in the midst of the goodness and brokenness of relationship, and ultimately to know that love never dies. With that in mind, three stories, stories about my parents, provide significant teachable moments that continue to challenge and transform me.

The first story: My mom, Elizabeth, a woman of deep faith, was diagnosed with an aggressive cancer at age fifty-three. Following two months of chemotherapy and hearing her doctor indicate that there were no more treatment options, she looked at my sister, Kathy, and me and said, "Let's go home, get things in order, and enjoy the time we have left together." These were words that we were not prepared to hear. Yet, in the midst of deep sadness and fear of the unknown, mom looked at us with love and said:

> Everything will be fine, I know where I'm going; heaven awaits me. It's time for me to go. My love will always be with you. I am so very proud of you two and your brothers. You have grown into wonderful people. I have a special love for each one of you and will love you forever. And, please, don't ever forget that we are family and that we love and care for and support each other always.

The second story: As my dad, Roger, stood over my hospital bed in the wake of my heart attack, I experienced a father's love for his firstborn and knew of his emotional connection with me in the tears that flowed from his eyes. He said: "My son, I love you. I don't want you to die." I responded: "I never knew that you loved me. I thought I was the son you never wanted, especially because I am so different from you." Without hesitation he replied, "I have always loved you, but you barely let me into your life; you have always kept me at a distance. Yes, we are different people and you have your particular gifts, but I allowed you to explore those gifts. I didn't hold you back." His statement literally rocked my world and the way I understood it. This conversation marked the beginning of a profound healing process in a father-son relationship; a process that I desired, but also feared.

Both my mom and dad taught me powerful life and faith lessons in these critical moments. I was challenged to see beyond the "goodness and brokenness" of their individual lives, of their married life, and of our familial life. I had to learn to trust more intimately in the power and presence of God, and to dare to let go of the need to control and orchestrate life.

As people of deep faith and trust in God, mom and dad opened the doors for me and my siblings not only to think about, but to ask for, forgiveness, healing, and reconciliation, which, of course, is challenging … yet so very life-giving in the end. As family, though making progress, we still have our issues and concerns – not to mention judgments about each other – as we continue to heal in the "goodness and brokenness" dynamic of life, love, and faith.

And here's the third story: A few days before her death, mom, from her hospital bed in the living room of our family home, asked dad to get her out of bed and to walk her to the kitchen for a drink of water. Time passed and I became concerned that something might have gone awry and that mom and dad needed assistance.

As I peered into the kitchen, I saw them in a tender embrace next to the sink. I overheard mom say to dad, "I want you to know you're the only man I've ever loved, and I will always love you." And then, as she and dad kissed and warmly embraced, mom became aware of my presence. She told me, in no uncertain terms, to mind my own business and allow them to have their special moment. My return to the family room was immediate and without hesitation. Yes, indeed, it was their special moment, a moment of healing, reconciliation, and expression of love and commitment.

Mom always told us kids that she took her marriage vows seriously . . . "in good times and in bad, in sickness and in health, until death do us part." Their example inspires me to this day.

Over time, I realized that my sojourn to heaven, coupled

with a reluctant return to earth, was and is about being a messenger of healing, reconciliation, and love from the inside out, that of a "wounded healer." Without a doubt, this is my ongoing mission and ministry as a man of faith and a priest of God. As I heal, reconcile, and love from the inside out, I am empowered to invite others to do the same. A personal willingness to do so is the best teacher and example to and for others. Actions do speak louder than words. Once again, mom was right.

Special moments in time with those whom we love are God's gifts to us. Such moments are filled with God's grace, renewing us in spirit and calling us to be people of faith-in-action. And, ultimately, graced moments in time propel us into deeper trust, faith, and companionship on life's journey.

CHAPTER SIX
the "what" and "where" of heaven

Heaven "is neither an abstraction nor a physical
place in the clouds, but a living, personal relationship
with the Holy Trinity."
(Pope John Paul II, 1999, General Audience)

Not only did I want my family at my side to comfort me
and heal my broken heart, I also desired to be in heaven. Only
with time, however, would I begin to understand that I was not
alone in my experience and desire. Many others have had near-
death experiences, and they, too, wanted family by their side,
while at the same time desiring to be in heaven with Jesus. The

Christian dilemma, then, is how to make sense of the experience of wanting two seemingly different realities, life and earth and life in heaven. But does such a choice have to be made? In this context, it seems appropriate to take a step back and look at, study, and contemplate the experiences and articulations of heaven from the writings of others: popular literature, Christian tradition, the teaching magisterium of the Roman Catholic Church, and Sacred Scripture.

A Time magazine article and three popular books - 90 *Minutes in Heaven*, *Heaven is for Real*, and *Five People You Meet in Heaven* - helped prepare me to share my journey to heaven, my conversation with Jesus, and my undesired return to the life on earth.

Author Jon Meacham (2012) in a Time magazine article titled "Heaven can't wait: Why rethinking the hereafter could make the world a better place," posed some rather provocative questions that create a powerful template through which to explore thoughts, ideas, and concepts about heaven. I found his presentation particularly inviting, affirming, and encouraging, as well as challenging. Here are Meacham's key thoughts, perspectives, and questions:

"Heaven isn't just a place you go. Heaven is how you live your life."

"What if Christianity is not about enduring this sinful, fallen world in search of a reward of eternal rest? What if the authors of the New Testament were actually talking about a bodily resurrection in which God brings together the heavens and the earth in a wholly new, wholly redeemed creation?"

"What if heaven is about "stewardship now?"

The essence of the Time magazine article can be summarized in a single statement. Simply, yet profoundly stated, Meacham says that heaven is "about whether believing Christians see earthly life as inextricably bound up with eternal life or as simply a prelude to a heavenly existence elsewhere" (p. 32). So, what if heaven and earth are not separate realities or experiences? What if they are one continuous reality for all eternity?

The Gospel writers Luke and Mark offer thought-provoking perspectives on the reality of heaven. Jesus proclaims in the Gospel of Luke (17:21b): "The Reign of God is already in your midst." And, in the Gospel of Mark (1:15), Jesus boldly preaches: "This is the time of fulfillment. The Reign of God is at hand! Reform your lives and believe in the gospel." Indeed, Jesus' words present powerful images and realities of heaven as he teaches about "reign" and "the time of fulfillment" as already present, already in our midst. Both the "Reign of God" and "the time of fulfillment" are here, but not fully, not completely.

If, indeed the Kingdom of Heaven is here in our midst, then there are powerful questions to ask and explore: Why are we waiting for the arrival of the Kingdom of Heaven if it's already here, though not fully or completely? What might we be missing, specifically not recognizing about Jesus' call to reform and re-form our lives, hearts, and minds, so as to believe and experience more fully the Reign, the Kingdom...the very reality of heaven in our midst?

"Reform your lives and believe in the Gospel," says Jesus. Yet, more often than not, we tend to resist "Reign," "Kingdom," and "Heaven" language in the bigger picture of our lives as individuals, families, and communities of faith. Nonetheless, Jesus challenges us to enter more deeply into the mystery and process of re-formation. He invites us to experience a complete change of heart - *metanoia* - inviting us to make right what we need to make right, to rethink and to re-form. And, not surprisingly, though most challenging perhaps, Jesus asks that we begin not with the incompleteness, fault, or sin of the other, but with ourselves. Why? Because re-formation, transformation, healing, and reconciliation - the making of and getting life and relationships "right" and more meaningful and peace-filled – happens from the inside out and begins in present time. It's about a true homecoming, the gathering of family, friends, and saints journeying into the fullness of the presence of God in the Kingdom that we know and call heaven. Heaven is about the fullness of life and unconditional love of God; it is about a journey into the fullness of life and love of God, a journey into the very heart of God.

In *90 Minutes in Heaven*, Baptist Pastor Don Piper (2004), having gone to heaven after a near fatal automobile crash with a semi-tractor trailer and returned to earth, describes heaven as "mystery and faith...the very presence of God...(that)...words cannot describe...(in the midst of a)...sensory explosion of sight, sound, and smell." In heaven, he says, "there is no need of any kind...no chaos...perfection and agelessness...no suffering or disease...in the presence of loved ones and angels." And, of course, he, like many others, tells of his strong desire to remain in heaven rather than return to earth.

Pastor Todd Burpo (2010), in *Heaven is for Real*, brings a child's perspective to the experience, understanding, and conception of heaven. Four-year-old Colton Burpo, Pastor Burpo's son who died as a result of acute appendicitis, describes his sojourn to heaven as one with "lots of color, people, and animals." He details powerful scenarios of "angels picking me up and singing to me" and of spending time "hanging out" with Jesus and the Holy Spirit. In heaven, recounts Colton, "no one is old . . . all have wings . . . and we get to meet up with family members." And, he, too, tells of his desire to remain in heaven; yet, like many others, he, too, had to return to life on earth.

In the fictional book, *The Five People You Meet In Heaven*, author Mitch Albom (2003) focuses on Eddie, an eighty-three-year-old man who gives his life to save a young girl at Ruby Pier where he serves as a maintenance man and amusement park ride operator. And, one day, actually his 83rd birthday, while operating one of Ruby Pier's most popular rides – *Freddy's Free Fall* – Eddie sees one of the ride carts break away and fall toward the ground, right in the direction of a young girl. Eddie rushes toward the girl to push her out of harm's way. He dies as a result of his sacrificial and lifesaving gesture, only to wake up in heaven.

Eddie was alone in life for many, many years and often wondered if life really mattered and, more specifically, if his life on earth made any difference to anyone. Once in heaven, he meets up with five influential people in his life: the Blue Man from the local circus, his military captain, Ruby of Ruby Pier, Marguerite his beloved wife, and Tala the young girl whose village he and his military platoon burned to the ground.

The Blue Man who gave his life for Eddie as a young boy teaches him that there are "no random acts in life." His military captain, reminds him that "no one gets left behind" in war or life. Ruby invites him to recognize, perhaps for the first time, that in his relationship with his father there was both "goodness and brokenness" and that he must look beneath the brokenness of his father's struggle with addiction – his alcoholism, specifically – to the goodness and love in his heart. Marguerite, Eddie's wife who died early in their marriage after a bout with cancer, responds to his question as to why she had to leave him alone, poignantly reminding him that "life ends, love doesn't." And, finally, Tala, the young girl burned to death in her village by Eddie and his military platoon, reminds him that "actions have importance," as she forgives him for what he had done as a young man.

Suddenly, as if in an instant, Eddie's life in heaven takes on new breath, depth, and perspective. He is at peace; he is reconciled, forgiven, and loved completely without conditions of any kind. Eddie is healed and freed from the inside out. What a powerful and re-creative reality open to all of us if only we desire, welcome, accept, and embrace it. Indeed, there is transformative power and grace in experiences of peace, reconciliation, forgiveness, healing, and love that do not have conditions of any kind.

The article from Time magazine on heaven (Meacham, 2012) and the books featuring Pastor Don Piper, Colton Burpo, and Eddie of Ruby Pier invite us to consider the Reign of God already in our midst. In doing so, we also recognize that the time of fulfillment is made manifest in the living, loving, and reconciling interactions that relationships invite and, in some cases, demand. It is nothing short of being good stewards of all that we are and have in God.

The "what" and "where" of heaven bespeak "a living personal relationship with the Holy Trinity" beginning here on earth as taught by Pope John Paul II (1999). Pope Benedict XVI (2007) added breadth and depth to our perspectives on heaven when he spoke of love and the afterlife:

> The belief that love can reach into the afterlife, that reciprocal giving and receiving is possible, in which our affection for one another continues beyond the limits of death—this has been a fundamental conviction of Christianity throughout the ages and it remains a source of comfort today. (48)

The Catechism of the Catholic Church (2012) addresses heaven in similar relational language. "Heaven is the ultimate end and fulfillment of the deepest human longings, the state of supreme, definitive happiness" (1024). Roman Catholic tradition and the teachings of the magisterium invite us to a mature adult understanding of heaven.

Thomas Merton, an Abbey of Gethsemani Trappist

monk and priest who was a prolific writer of the twentieth century, as well as a poet, mystic, social activist, and an avidly dedicated learner and scholar of comparative religion, invites us, too, to a mature adult faith and understanding of heaven. In his work, *Seeds of Contemplation*, Merton (1948) explores heaven as love:

> God is a consuming fire. If we, by love become transformed into God and burn as God burns, God's fire will be our everlasting joy. When we love God we find joy in all things. We are one with God and others. (p. 75)

The Torah (the first five books of the Old Testament) does not address, define, or set forth a clear understanding of life after death, either in individual or communal terms. Our ancestors in faith focused on living a faithful covenant relationship with God here on earth; they didn't have a precise concept or understanding of life after death. That developed over time through the centuries.

For Christians, life, death, and eternal life have meaning and perspective in time and eternity because of the Paschal Mystery. As highlighted by several descriptors of *The Catechism of the Catholic Church*, heaven is "our true homeland" (2802). And the journey into the fullness of heaven is further described as "perfect life...communion of life and love...the ultimate end and fulfillment of our deepest longings" (1024), "blessed communion" (1027), and "life light and peace"(1027) beyond all human imagination.

Heaven is ultimately a mystery of faith. And, as we know, mystery is not to be solved, but entered into and lived in trust and confidence that God is Creator, for "in the beginning...God created the heavens and the earth..." and, indeed it was and is very good (Genesis 1:1). Life, death, and eternal life - heaven and earth - form one great mystery of God's infinite goodness to us from the beginning of creation. And we recognize in this great mystery of life and love that "there is an appointed time for everything, and a time for every affair under the heavens." (Ecclesiastes 3:1)

In the final analysis, the reality of death - the temporal nature and fragility of life - gives a profound sense of urgency to our lives. This is evidenced by a resolve to live from the heart, knowing that there is an appointed time for everything, most especially, faithfulness and fidelity to the mission of Jesus Christ in which we all share by virtue of our baptism. By baptism, we have been claimed for Jesus Christ; and, confirmed in faith, we participate fully and intimately in the Paschal Mystery. We live, suffer, and die, so as to be reborn again; such is the mystery of our faith.

Reflection: The "what" and "where" of Heaven

"The reign of God is already in your midst." (Luke 17:21b)

"This is the time of fulfillment. The reign of God is at hand! Reform your lives and believe in the gospel." (Mark 1:15)

The *Catechism of the Catholic Church* offers several descriptors of heaven. Heaven is:
- "Beyond our imagination" (n. 1027)
- "Perfect communion" (n. 1024)
- "The ultimate end and fulfillment of our deepest longings" (n. 1024)
- "Perfect love" (n. 1024)
- "Our true homeland" (n. 2802)
- "Light . . . life-changing experience of the living God" (n. 1027)

What have you been taught about heaven?

_____

_____

_____

_____

_____

_____

_____

"Heaven isn't just a place you go, heaven is how you live your life." (Jon Meacham, TIME, April 16, 2012) Reflect on what this statement means to you. Do you agree?

_____

_____

_____

_____

_____

_____

_____

_____

_____

_____

_____

_____

_____

_____

_____

_____

_____

_____

_____

_____

What do you think about heaven demanding stewardship in "present time?" What might that mean in your daily living and relating with others?

_____

_____

_____

_____

_____

_____

_____

_____

_____

_____

_____

_____

_____

_____

_____

_____

_____

_____

_____

_____

If "heaven isn't a place you go, but how you live your life,"
what needs to shift or change in your understanding and expression of Christian faith?

_____

_____

_____

_____

_____

_____

_____

_____

_____

_____

_____

_____

_____

_____

_____

_____

_____

_____

_____

_____

Merton, Pope St. John Paul II, the Catechism of the Catholic Church, as well as Pope Emeritus Benedict XVI speak of heaven as "relationship" grounded in love with the Holy Trinity, the Communion of Saints, and our fellow human beings. What needs to change, be healed, and/or forgiven in your life today so that you can continue to progress into "perfect communion?"

_____

_____

_____

_____

_____

_____

_____

_____

_____

_____

_____

_____

_____

_____

_____

_____

_____

_____

_____

_____

Who are the five people you would like to meet in heaven?

1. _____

2. _____

3. _____

4. _____

5. _____

What LESSON would each person teach you about life, love, relationship, faith, etc.?

1. _____

2. _____

3. _____

4. _____

5. _____

CHAPTER SEVEN
body and soul reunited

"I call the soul 'heaven' because I make heaven wherever I dwell by grace.
I made the soul my hiding place and by my love
turned her into a mansion."
(Catherine of Siena, 1980, p. 75)

With my spirit - my soul - and physical body united once again, I found myself listening attentively to the young doctor at my side. He told me that I had experienced a major heart attack and that I would need to be airlifted to Presbyterian Hospital in Albuquerque. The transport, however, could not take place before my blood pressure was stabilized; it was elevated as a result of the cardiac event, and continued to be so, primarily because of my anxiety and fear.

The doctor encouraged me to relax as he held my hand in a gesture of comfort, calm, and I suppose human compassion, which, of course, I didn't much like. In that moment I somehow knew I needed to begin to do things differently, to live life from the inside out. The first step, I thought, was to trust in the goodness of another human being, to allow someone into my space so as to express care and concern, even if that person was a complete stranger. So I allowed the doctor to continue holding my hand.

Time seemed to move at a snail's pace, but eventually my blood pressure stabilized. In the interim, I asked the ER staff to contact my dad, Roger, my sister, Kathy, and my New Mexico family, Peter and Shirley Vigil and Gilbert and Theresa Cruz, as well as friends from the parish in Clovis. Not long thereafter, I was informed that my dad and sister would travel to Albuquerque as soon as possible, that Peter, Shirley, Gilbert, and Theresa were on their way to Albuquerque from Holman, some two-and-a-half hours away, and that my Clovis friends were praying for me.

Several hours later, accompanied by a medical team and pilot, I was on my way to Albuquerque. I recall landing at the airport and the ambulance transport to the hospital emergency room. A seasoned cardiologist greeted me there, and he didn't seem thrilled to have been called to work in the early hours of the morning. With a smile on his face, he told me that his Catholic wife, an RN by profession, made him answer the call because "a young priest had a heart attack." He indicated that he would take me on as a patient, but only if I would do what he asked of me. I agreed without hesitation.

Once I was settled in an emergency room cubicle, my dear friends – my New Mexican family – Peter and Shirley Vigil and Gilbert and Theresa Cruz were at my bedside. It was an emotional reunion. As Peter stood looking down at me, I recall a tear from his eye drop on my hospital gown, which of course got my attention, as I had not experienced this side of him ever before. I was unsure of what to say or how to respond, but before I could say or do anything, he said: "You can't die on me now. You're my friend and I love you. You're family." Shirley nodded her head in agreement as she clasped Peter's hand, placing her other hand on my shoulder in a gesture of friendship, love, and healing. Gilbert and Theresa expressed similar thoughts and feelings. Moreover, all agreed that I couldn't die yet because we were in the middle of building a cabin for me. I was deeply aware of their love for me and profoundly grateful to have them as family at my side.

My dad and sister arrived late in the afternoon the following day. It was yet another emotional reunion. Dad was visibly shaken as he stood in the doorway of the hospital room, while Kathy didn't hesitate to enter and warmly greet me with a warm hug and a kiss, and her customary, "I love you, John." I knew, too, that dad cared and was afraid for me; his teary eyes told me so.

I was scheduled for an angioplasty the following day, as a heart catheterization confirmed a ninety-five percent blockage in my right coronary artery. Prepared for open-heart surgery in the event on an unsuccessful procedure, I was transported to the operating room. I observed the procedure on a monitor mounted on the ceiling, encouraged by the doctor's running medical evaluation and commentary. Before I knew it, I was back in my hospital room on the cardiac floor with specific instructions not to move until the femoral vein opening in my upper leg was no longer in danger of severe bleeding.

There was ample time to rest, enjoy the many, many floral arrangements and green plants that had been sent to my room by family and friends, and to receive visitors. Or so I thought. In reality, I was not resting much at all because a steady stream of visitors was arriving at the hospital. This raised concerns for the medical team caring for me and, on day two of my hospital stay, they limited the number of guests and requested that dad and Kathy monitor all visitors and the many incoming phone calls. Dad and Kathy, both of them extremely social by nature, rose to the occasion, providing everyone with daily updates and prognosis. Of course, people like Archbishop Michael Sheehan, Fr. Joel Garner, O. Praem., and the

Norbertine Community, along with some close friends, both lay and clergy, passed through the visitor screening process without incident. In the end, I did get the rest I needed for initial recovery and healing.

I remained hospitalized for about a week. Upon discharge, I took up residence with the Norbertine Community in Albuquerque. The warm and generous invitation to reside, rest, and heal with them came at an opportune time. However, being with them felt somewhat awkward in light of the fact that I had left the Norbertine Order several years prior to incardinate into the Archdiocese of Santa Fe; that is, to become a diocesan priest. Yet, as I would come to know in a deeper way, the bond of brotherhood - the bond of fraternity - established many years prior with the Norbertine Community was still strong and meaningful.

The time I spent with the Norbertine Community was healing and life-giving. Additionally, my participation in a medically based holistic health program got me out of the house daily for several weeks to engage in various exercise, nutrition, cooking, and self-improvement classes, not to mention ample opportunity to interact and socialize with others in heart-healing activities. Most importantly, I quit smoking and began to exercise daily and eat healthily. Admittedly, the most challenging aspect of the healing process was the amount of quiet time afforded me as part of the holistic health program. Though

I ended up in a place I did not want to be, face-to-face with my broken heart, I slowly began to see light and experience healing and new life as evidenced by a growing resolve to live and relate with deeper integrity; that is, with honesty and in freedom and peace.

CHAPTER EIGHT
profound healing and transformation begin

"We strive to picture heaven, when we are barely at the
threshold of the inconceivable beauty of earth."
(Higginson, 1897, p. 28)

I decided to renew my spiritual life - my personal prayer
life in particular - in light of the significant time afforded me
during the healing process post cardiac event. As you might
imagine, I was so attuned to "being busy" that I struggled with
simply "being." Though challenging, I stayed the course and
increased quiet time for prayer each day. Additionally, I began
to reflect upon what I could and would do to gain a more positive self-image.

One day as I was reading and reflecting upon the beginning of Jesus' public ministry, specifically his proclamation of the ancient words of the prophet Isaiah in his hometown synagogue among those whom he loved, I experienced a moment of clarity and insight. They are words I read and heard proclaimed many times, but words that now took on deeper meaning and significance:

> The spirit of the Lord is upon me, because he has anointed me to bring glad tidings to the poor. He has sent me to proclaim liberty to captives and recovery of sight to the blind, to let the oppressed go free, and to proclaim a year acceptable to the Lord. (Luke 4:18-19)

I have always known that "the spirit of the Lord is upon me" and that my life was to be spent in service of others, especially those most in need. But little did I realize I would first have to proclaim liberty and freedom to myself in order to serve others well and to invite them into the freedom of healthy and holy living and loving.

"What does proclaiming liberty and freedom mean and what would it look like in my life?," I thought. "What 'glad tidings' do I need to hear in my poverty and brokenness?" And,

"In what ways am I blind, oppressed, and held captive? For what freedom or freedoms in 'a year acceptable to the Lord' do I long, or need to move toward in my daily life, work, and ministry?" I wasn't sure in the moment, but I did know that something had to change.

My broken heart was a tangible sign of the fundamental experience and reality with which I had lived from young days onward: the feeling of "being flawed," of being "damaged goods," of not being good enough or smart enough to be noteworthy in the schema of life and faith. I had mastered the art of how to play it small and safe in the midst of tumultuous and uncertain family dynamics and relationships-at-large. I learned to live out of a pervasive fear of life itself, especially fear of that which I could not manage or control. Moreover, I often felt paralyzed before the world, as best evidenced by a deep-seeded fear of public speaking and interaction with others. I avoided most social settings as well. After all, "What did I have to offer the world?" "Not much," I thought for many, many years.

But, nevertheless, I knew then - but did not really believe, trust, and act upon it - and continue to know now - believing, trusting, and acting upon it more so than ever - that the Lord has always been and continues with me; I don't journey alone. Perhaps that's the seed of my vocational call to service, religious life, priesthood, and deeper personal integrity that grows stronger day by day. In the words of the prophet

Jeremiah (1:4-10):

> The word of the Lord came to me thus: Before I formed you in the womb I knew you, before you were born I dedicated you, a prophet to the nations I appointed you. "Ah, Lord God!" I said, "I know not how to speak; I am too young. But the Lord answered me. Say not, "I am too young." To whomever I send you, you shall go; whatever I command you, you shall speak. Have no fear before them, because I am with you to deliver you, says the Lord. Then the Lord extended his hand and touched my mouth saying, see, I place my words in your mouth! This day I set you over nations and over kingdoms, to root up and to tear down, to destroy and to demolish, to build and to plant.

As I heal and become stronger and more confident from the inside out like the prophet Jeremiah, my fears and personal shortcomings are not eliminated. Rather, they are transformed into experiences and realities of strength that continue to support and encourage others on a similar spiritual journey of faith-filled growth and development. Only as I continue to move through my inner blindness and oppression, embracing all that is acceptable to the Lord, am I able to be a source of encouragement and a fellow peregrino with others who dare to step into and share more fully and completely in Jesus' mission. Yes, indeed, God's words have been placed in my mouth and upon my heart. The same is true in your life and Christian service as well.

So, what about not being good or smart enough? And, what about the fear of public speaking? Both are still with me, of course, but they are no longer paralyzing realities that halt or limit me in daily life and ministry. From childhood I internalized a message of not being good enough or smart enough to succeed in life. For example, I wasn't good enough to be on the football team at school, or for that matter, to excel in any sport. I was the fat kid who never got picked for the team, always wrestling with not fitting in or being able to fulfill the expectations of others. I was also told by a high school teacher/counselor that I wasn't smart enough to attend college. And, in college, an esteemed professor told me that I had extremely poor writing skills and didn't measure up to other priests who were much better writers than I.

Simply, for years I wasn't part of the "in" crowd on any count. In a bit of irony, though, the aforemenitoned perceived weaknesses have become my greatest strengths. And, perhaps most importantly, God has consistently called me to an ongoing personal transformation that continues to forge a life and ministry grounded in confidence, humility, excellence, and justice. In short, I have found my voice, and for this great gift I am extremely grateful.

The seeds of spiritual transformation took root and began to grow in the fertile soil of my broken heart as I embraced recovery during my time with the Norbertine Community. Recovery continued, too, as I returned to active parish ministry at Our Lady of Guadalupe Parish in Clovis some three months later. The church community received me warmly and was sensitive to my need slowly to reengage in life and ministry. I felt unsure, unstable, and personally "bankrupt" to function in public as priest, however. This reality perplexed and deeply disturbed me. My energies were being spent on a profoundly transformative interior journey of faith that felt like an excruciating dark night of the soul, but one I trusted would bear fruit, light, and new insight over time. But when would that time arrive?

In the meantime, and upon the recommendation of my cardiologist, I requested a medical leave of absence from active ministry as a priest from Archbishop Michael Sheehan. My request was denied, due in large part to a diminished number of active clergy in the Archdiocese at that time. I clearly recall the archbishop's words to me: "You're a good man and priest, John. I need you in a parish. If you're meant to die in the saddle, then that is what's meant to be." I immediately tendered a two-week verbal notice of resignation, to which the archbishop responded, "John, priests don't give notices of resignation." I replied: "Well, archbishop, with all due respect, I believe I just gave you a verbal notice. I will vacate the parish in two weeks and notify you so that you can appoint a new pastor." I then excused myself and left the archbishop's office and drove home to Clovis.

Two weeks later, I called the archbishop's secretary and informed her that I was vacating the parish. I then got into my vehicle and embarked on a new and daunting adventure. There was a sense of freedom and relief as I drove away from the parish complex. Yes, there was a sense of excitement, but also frustration, anger, and deep sadness that I wasn't granted the medical leave of absence I so desired and needed. With all of my earthly possessions in my vehicle, I drove into a new and undetermined future that did not include the priesthood.

My destination was Northern New Mexico, to live up the hill from my dear friends Peter and Shirley in the cabin they were helping me to build. In order to pay the bills, I took a job as a dorm counselor at a residential treatment center for challenged teenagers. A few months later, realizing that I was unfulfilled as a dorm counselor, and strongly encouraged by conversation with the clinical director of the treatment center, Linda Romero, LISW, I began to explore the master level

Social Work program at Highlands University in Las Vegas, NM. After all, what kind of fulfilling job, living, and money could I make with an undergraduate degree in Sociology and a graduate degree in Theology? I jokingly, though realistically, concluded that I couldn't even buy a cup of coffee and a newspaper with said degrees in hand. I needed meaningful and gainful employment, "something more," to make it in the world . . . or so I thought.

Much to my amazement, that "something more" would include a return to active ministry as a priest and a course of study at Highlands University. For two years I made the commute twice weekly from San Francisco Asís Parish in Ranchos de Taos to Highlands University in Las Vegas. I completed my Master of Social Work degree in 1997, and did so with academic honors.

Concerned that my life might be shorter than longer – after all, I had had a major heart attack – I decided to maximize my potential, my God-given talent, by exploring secular employment. I was convinced, once again, that I would depart from active ministry as a priest – this time permanently. My departure from active ministry as a priest was quiet and uneventful, as was my transition to the clinical team and ultimate clinical directorship at the aforementioned residential teen treatment center. My Social Work career eventually led to a very successful private counseling practice in Santa Fe and a course of study at the University of Phoenix campus in Albuquerque where I studied business. I was graduated with honors with a Master's in Business Administration (MBA) in 2003.

I was a man of faith on a mission. The spirit of the Lord was upon me. Life was good, albeit not neatly wrapped or packaged. Healing and internal transformation continued. My confidence increased and my sight - my insight - continued to develop as well. It was unmistakably evident that I was gaining increased freedom from deep-seated historical fears and my sense of personal inadequacy.

Though initially reluctant to return to earth, and rather confused after my heart attack, I now had a greater clarity of mission and the desire to embrace my life more completely, both personally and professionally. I wanted to live *now*, more than ever!

Reflection: In the spirit of
Jeremiah the Prophet

What is your favorite Scripture passage?

_____

_____

_____

Why is it your favorite Scripture passage?

_____

_____

_____

_____

_____

_____

_____

_____

_____

_____

_____

_____

_____

CHAPTER NINE

stories of healing and homecoming

"But I believe I shall enjoy the Lord's goodness
in the land of the living."
(Psalm 27:13)

I am convinced that this chapter of stories about healing
and homecoming is the heart and soul of this book. It is not by
chance, then, that this chapter is the longest and most detailed. I
share with you several personal stories of faith, love, and commitment, as well as stories of healing and reconciliation that
propel me and hopefully you, too, into the very mystery of our
triune God. For it is God who created us and allows creative

energy to renew – to transform us – each and every day, Jesus who redeems us, calling us to die to sin and self so that we might live in freedom and without fear, and the Holy Spirit who sanctifies us, declaring us worthy, holy, and ready for a mission filled with hope. It is with honor and humility that I share these stories of family, faith, and friendship with you.

I have three younger siblings: Roger Jr., Kathy, and Jim. There is a ten-year age difference between Jim and me. Each sibling has married, one has experienced divorce, and all have children. Roger Jr. and Kathy are also grandparents; and, they live near the family home in Escanaba, MI, while Jim and his family live near Rochester, NY. Typical family dynamics have always been at work among us, much like within any family system.

We four Tourangeau siblings are survivors and each is rather strongly opinionated and determined. Certainly this has presented challenges and difficulties between and among us over the years. Yet, we have healed and reconciled, at least enough to be able to be together and behave appropriately at family functions and gatherings. There is room, too, for ongoing healing and reconciliation which can only be realized as each of us does his or her own interior work in support of growth and development within the wider familial context. For sure, growth and change at both individual and relational levels have to begin at "home," not by pointing a finger of judgment at the "other" demanding that they change first.

Often when I think of my mom, I recall that her favorite Scripture reading was *Psalm 27*. She lived united with the Lord in both good and not so good times, in times of happiness and health, as well as in the darkness of depression and cancer, until death beckoned her from this life to the fullness of eternal life.

Like the divinely inspired great King David with his large and heavy human clay feet, mom held fast to the Lord as her stronghold. Pursued by adversaries, shunned and excluded by some, and subject to judgment, gossip, and perhaps even slander, she maintained confidence in God as her rock of hope, recognizing and teaching us about the power of prayer, faith, and communion with God. Indeed, *Psalm 27* was her song of light and hope, of "the good things of the Lord."

> The Lord is my light and my salvation;
>   whom should I fear?
> The Lord is my life's refuge;
>   of whom should I be afraid?
> One thing I ask of the Lord; this I seek:
> To dwell in the house of the Lord all the days of
>   my life,
> To gaze on the Lord's beauty, to visit his temple.
> Hear my voice, Lord, when I call;

have mercy on me and answer me.

Do not hide your face from me;

> do not repel your servant in anger.

You are my help; do not cast me off;

> do not forsake me, God my savior!.

But I believe I shall enjoy the Lord's goodness in

> the land of the living.

Wait for the Lord, take courage;

> be stouthearted, wait for the Lord!

Mom always believed that she would see the good things of the Lord in the land of the living; she possessed an unparalleled trust in God. And even though deemed "weak," (i.e. "ineffective," and "mentally ill") by some, mom was filled with deep faith, courage, and determination as she lived her life and faith.

Stouthearted, indeed, my mom was a woman who had her priorities in order: God was her cornerstone, followed by family, and community. She was determined, brave, courageous, bold, and valiant in the midst of life's challenges, struggles, and uncertainties. This is the woman, the young mother of two little boys who, in her twenties, while hospitalized at an institution in a catatonic state, compelled herself to reconnect with her inner spirit and then, subsequently, with the world around her. All this so that she could avoid further electric shock therapy and a potential lobotomy, the one-time common neurosurgical procedure to treat "mental disorders" like severe major depression.

Mom told me about her long mental health hospitalization not long before her untimely death in 1989 at the age of fifty-three. Moreover, in that moment of darkness and sheer helplessness, she recounted with great detail her decision to choose life from that moment on. She spoke about the interior steps from the prison of catatonia to a homecoming to self and family not thought possible by many. She vowed, too, in that moment, never to return to the State Hospital, or to take medication of any kind, though I suspect doing so may have helped her to some degree. And through it all, she never departed from healthy relationship with the God. Though not perfect, life was good; mom's faith ultimately sustained her.

Mom miraculously returned home and never was institutionalized again. Her desire was always to dwell in the house of the Lord; it is where she always placed her heart and where she now lives for all eternity. She taught my siblings and me to do the same.

In mid-August 1974, with the family station wagon carefully packed with my personal belongings, mom, dad, Grandma

Kutches, my siblings, and I were on our way to St. Lawrence Seminary in Mt. Calvary, WI. I don't recall much of that first trip from home to the boarding high school; yet, what I do recall from that trip was our stopping at several picturesque rural Wisconsin Catholic churches along State Highway 57 and our taking time for a picnic lunch at one of them. Mom, of course, would not miss an opportunity to offer a prayer and ask God's blessing upon the family and those in need. I suspect that a new prayer intention was added that day for me, her firstborn, who was leaving home. Life would be different now; home would not be the same.

We arrived at St. Lawrence and mom and dad helped me get settled in the dormitory. I had a bed and a small locker for clothes and personal items, certainly much less space than at home, but it didn't seem to bother me. We said our goodbyes amidst hugs, kisses, and, yes, some tears. I sat atop the large rock in front of Main Hall and watched mom and dad drive off. "What have I gotten myself into?," I thought. I suddenly felt alone and unsettled, perhaps even somewhat scared and dreadful of the upcoming afternoon football practice. Why did I agree to be on the football team? I wasn't good at it, nor did I even like sports.

Wrapped in a tapestry of emotions, I jumped from the top of the aforementioned rock and headed to the dorm to unpack my belongings and get settled. As I walked toward my bed, I noticed another young man sitting at the foot of his bed. I introduced myself to him and he did the same in return. We were both new to the boarding school family and beginning our third year of high school. We were both early arrivals, too, for football training camp. He was much more excited, though, than I. Tom Koene and I became friends that day, a friendship that survives the ebb and flow of both good and challenging times.

The time I spent at St. Lawrence was momentous and meaningful. Those two years were critical years of formation. I was challenged to grow academically, personally, and interpersonally. I learned good study habits that I believe opened the door to serious consideration of college, vocation, career, and Christian service, especially among the poor and disenfranchised.

I continue to learn from both past and present experiences, from the good as well as challenging and more difficult moments. Time, coupled with more mature faith, adds perspective and offers the opportunity for ongoing healing, reconciliation, and forgiveness, especially forgiveness of self for past transgressions and errors that have hurt others as well as myself. Learning to let go, forgive, heal, reconcile, and get on with living and loving is important, though admittedly, a life-long process.

Perhaps the most significant individual in my life has been my paternal uncle, Clem, one of my dad's older brothers. Uncle Clem was a simple man, a man of deep and abiding faith; a saint in my eyes and in the eyes of many others, as well. He was not only a man of deep prayer and trust in God, but also a profound example of Christian humility as a Religious Order brother and member of St. Norbert Abbey and family member. Moreover, Uncle Clem was a sturdy and steady figure in my life as I grew up.

The one special memory my cousins and I have of Uncle Clem is his annual summer visits home to the Tourangeau family dairy farm in Flatrock, near Escanaba, MI. We would spend time together with him, enjoying and learning from his gentle, loving, and encouraging manner.

Without fail, Clem would always gather us for an all-day bike ride through the countryside, ending at the family homestead where only remnants of a stone house foundation remained. There we would sit in the tall grass, share a hearty picnic lunch prepared by Uncle Clem and several of our mothers, and listen to the stories of generational family life and faith with great enthusiasm. Clem was a mainstay and stellar figure in our lives; he bought faith, hope, and a sense of stability to our family life.

Uncle Clem, faithful friend of Jesus that he was, always

prayed for us as we navigated the contours of daily living, loving, and relating. His example called – and continues to call – us to greater faithfulness and fidelity in matters of life and faith. And, he never judged anyone to the best of my knowledge; and, he always prayed for a deeper sense of conversion and fidelity, first for himself, then for others.

Dad began to mellow and change as a result of two major life events: the death of mom in July1989 and my cardiac event in1993. Perhaps there are other significant events as well, but these are two of which I am acutely aware.

In death, dad realized anew the blessings of his marriage to mom, even mixed with all of the uncertainties and challenges. Early on, dad would sit in his lawn chair at Holy Cross Cemetery, the site of mom's grave, wishing that it all could have had a different outcome. But with time came healing; eventually, dad was able to visit the cemetery without his lawn chair.

In the midst of our own grieving process, we siblings encouraged dad to forgive himself as mom forgave him prior to her death, and to get on with life. Mom had not only forgiven dad, but also "freed" dad to remarry; that is, mom gave him permission to do so, though he didn't actually need it. And, dad did remarry four years after mom's death. Betty, our stepmom, along with her adult children, Greg Dittrich and Kim Bigley and their spouses and children, have been a wonderful addition to our family. Hopefully, we've been like additions to their family as well.

My cardiac event was also another powerful reminder of how quickly life and relationships can change without a moment's notice, a potent reminder to all of us to live as fully and completely as humanly possible in present time. For sure, living as fully and completely as humanly possible in present time can be rather challenging, even daunting. Let me tell two stories that demonstrate this reality: one about a favorite aunt and uncle and another about a gathering of my immediate family at the family home.

It was Christmas 1997, I believe. I had departed from active ministry as a priest earlier that year and begun full-time work as a clinical social worker. I had also purchased a new-to-me truck about the same time. Not having been able to celebrate Christmas with my family in Upper Michigan for many years, I decided to take vacation time and drive cross-country to surprise them. It would be great to be with family for the holidays.

I made the long trek from New Mexico to the UP in record time - two long days of extensive driving. It was Christmas Eve around dinnertime when I pulled into Escanaba; and, knowing that several extended family members typically gathered at an aunt and uncle's home for the holiday celebration, and knowing that my sister and brother and their families would be there as well, I decided to stop by to surprise everyone.

My uncle was delighted to see me. My aunt, on the other hand, didn't share his sentiment. Her discomfort at my unannounced arrival was something that I sensed immediately. My uncle's invitation to "come in" was not an invitation that my aunt seemed to desire. Long story short, an unanticipated and uncomfortable interaction at the front door of their home was challenging for the three of us. Yet, my uncle's graciousness-in-the-moment will always be remembered and appreciated. He welcomed me into their home after the uncomfortable initial front door encounter. I greeted everyone, shared some Christmas cheer, and sat with the children in the kitchen and enjoyed wonderful conversation with them, as well as some very good food. My niece and nephews were delighted and very excited to see me.

I got up from the small children's table in the kitchen after dinner, peered into the dining room where the adults were gathered at table, and thanked everyone for the evening. Wishing everyone a "Merry Christmas," I excused myself and drove the short distance to dad's house, where I enjoyed the rest of the evening in quite solitude until dad and Betty got home from Christmas Eve Mass.

My aunt has always been a favorite relative; yet, our relationship is not what it once was and continues to be framed by what I perceive and experience as a cordial distance. Would that we could have the opportunity to talk about what occurred between us, if anything, so as to shift our feelings and thoughts about each other. Perhaps she was and continues to be challenged by my life's course…my life's questions, challenges, uncertainties, struggles, and decisions. I'm really not sure. Certainly, I would have liked and would like my life to be in a neatly wrapped package, one that contains a socially acceptable and uneventful timeline. But that's not my life, nor, I believe, is it the reality of anyone's life.

I think of my aunt and uncle often. They are good people; yet, humanity, I believe, has come between us. And this reality has separated and distanced us for several years. I'm waiting for them - specifically for my aunt - to make the first move toward conversation, toward healing and reconciliation, if that's what needed, though I'm really not sure. And, I suspect that she's waiting for me, on the other hand. I have work to do for sure. I pray for the grace, humility, insight, and courage to take the first step, sooner than later. My aunt and uncle are very good people, indeed, and I miss them in my life every day.

A few days after the Christmas Eve event at my aunt and

uncle's home, my immediate family gathered at the family home to celebrate Christmas. Dad indicated that Roger Jr. was upset and that he would not come with his family if I were going to be at home. Dad confronted Roger and drew a parental line in the sand, indicating that he could make whatever choice he needed to make, but that I was family - that I was son and brother - and always welcome at home, regardless of any differences between us. Dad clearly communicated to him that "we are family, and all are welcome." What a profound statement of parental wisdom. Thank you, dad. Roger Jr. and his family did show up for the family Christmas celebration; we were all on our best behavior and managed sibling tension more appropriately than not.

Reconciliation with my brother, Roger Jr., came several years later at a Tourangeau family reunion in 2007, and it was because of his initiative, not mine. He took the "high road," approaching me at the gathering, saying "Hello, John. Good to see you. I know you like Tecate beer. There's a cooler in my SUV along with limes and salt. Help yourself whenever you want one. I got it for you." There you have it. What a great gesture of reconnection and of being family. This was his way of moving beyond what was distancing us. No formal apologies, only a powerful gesture of welcome, hospitality, and unconditional love.

In this context I'm also mindful of the kindness and generosity of my Norbertine brothers David Komatz, John Bostwick, and Dane Radecki. Having departed from the Norbertine Order in 1989 and moving to Mora, New Mexico, as diocesan pastor of St. Gertrude parish, I thought it important and necessary to establish and maintain some distance between religious and diocesan life, including friendships. While on a cross-country trip, Norbertines David and John made their way to Mora to visit me, affirming that formal organizational relationships may change, but that friendship does not. Indeed, friendship survives as temporal changes unfold; a reality for which I remain grateful! David and John, and later Dane, taught me about the importance and intimacy of friendship, fraternity, and brotherhood.

Dane has remained a brother and friend since my entrance into the Norbertine Order in 1978. He served early on as my spiritual director, challenging me in particular to grow into and develop a faith life firmly grounded in the fullness of the Paschal Mystery. He encouraged a faith in me firmly grounded in the life, suffering, death, and resurrection of Jesus Christ. Specifically, he challenged me to "get off the cross" and find some joy in daily living. "Faith," said Dane, "is more than the cross; we all suffer, but that's not what life is ultimately about."

How right he was. It is in the light, peace, and freedom of "resurrection" that life, suffering, and death take on new meaning. In other words, the "cross" is not the end. Life can be good; indeed, life is very good.

And speaking of the goodness of life, I think of my enduring friendship with the Vigil family. I've already spoken of my encounter with Peter and Shirley at my emergency room bedside in Albuquerque, yet there is so much more. I have known the Vigils for over twenty-five years and consider myself a member of their family, as they do me.

I first met Shirley at the organ in church where she was directing the Youth Choir at St. Gertrude's, all while eight months pregnant with their youngest child, Sarah María. And, I first met Peter at a Chacón workday - one of the missions of St. Gertrude's - where I approached him to bum a cigarette. Peter was impressed with my Spanish and wondered out loud to his buddy who the "gringo" was. He was surprised to learn that I was the new pastor. Little did we realize in these encounters what depth of love and friendship would result.

The Vigils have graciously and unconditionally welcomed me into the intimacy of their family. I am "Uncle John" to their four children: Jeanette, Vanessa, Anthony, and Sarah María. I have also been welcomed into their families, and have had the honor and privilege of witnessing their marriages, baptizing their children, and burying their grandparents, specifically, Shirley's dad and mom, Fidel and Hazel, and Peter's mom, Regina, or "Reggie," as she was affectionately known.

Our friendship and being family was affirmed in a significant way by an unexpected and generous gift as I was moving from St. Gertrude's in Mora to my new ministry assignment as pastor of Our Lady of Guadalupe Parish in Clovis: a plot of land on which to build a house, a place to call "home." Together we labored and made sacrifices to complete the construction of "The Cabin" begun in 1993 and completed some three years later, a sacred place that I continue to enjoy today. Indeed, I am greatly blessed to be part of their family.

Heavenly gifts, often unexpected and at times from the least likely of people, experiences, and circumstances, are true signs of God's loving presence and hope at work among us. Two formative and significant stories come to mind in this context, one about a life lesson in humility and another that underscores the experience of failure as the doorway to new opportunity.

The story about humility. Not long after my ordination to the priesthood, I had the occasion to visit my family for the weekend and to preside at Sunday Masses at my home parish since the pastor was away on vacation. The customary Sunday afternoon meal followed, a meal lovingly prepared and served by mom. Everyone enjoyed the meal, including the good conversation and laughter around extended time at table. As mom was putting away the leftover food and my siblings were preparing to do the dishes, dad looked at me in my new black dress suit and Roman collar and said, "John, you don't have to do dishes today; you've already put in a good day's work. Sit in my rocking chair and relax."

I felt as though I had arrived; I received an offer to sit in dad's rocking chair, his "throne" in which nobody dared to sit. So, without hesitation, I sat down, extended the footrest, pushed back in the chair, and prepared for a relaxing afternoon rest. But much to my surprise, mom suddenly appeared before me and said: "What do you think you're doing?" I proudly and confidently replied, "Dad said I don't have to do dishes today." And, with loving eyes and firmness in her voice, she said, "I don't care what your dad said. I'm your mother and you will listen to me. Now, I'm very proud of you and thank God that we have a priest in the family; however, you need to learn that before you're a priest, you're a 'son' and 'brother,' a member of this family. So, take off your priest shirt and get to the kitchen sink. You're doing dishes like everyone else." Dad said nothing, but I did note that he cracked a bit of a smile and winked at me. Without hesitation, question, or fanfare, I assumed my position at the kitchen sink and began washing.

Mom was right. I'm a son first, a brother second, and a

priest third. This lesson in humility was not only a powerful parental teaching moment, but continues to serve as a lifelong lesson that informs my thinking processes and actions. Whenever I'm tempted to play the "priest card" of privilege, I hear mom's voice calling me to humility and companionship with others – to true brotherhood – on life's journey. Mom always reminded us when we were together: "I'm proud of each of you and thank God and pray for you every day. No two of you are alike. God has made each of you special, and I'm so proud of who each of you is becoming in life."

My sister Kathy, too, carries on in mom's spirit when she needs to, saying "Well, here's my son the priest," mimicking in a good and humorous way mom's love and admiration of me. With a smile and twinkle in her eye, my sister invites me to the kitchen sink on a regular basis to engage in the sibling task of dishwashing. At times, I have to remind her, as I had to remind mom, that my name is "John," not "Father." After all, I'm a brother and a son before all else.

Now for the story about failure. It is about the gift of failure as it relates to my high school study of the French language. My grandparents, both paternal and maternal, were immigrants to North America from French-speaking Canada and the former Yugoslavia, respectively. French was my father's first language and Croatian was my mother's. They learned English attending Catholic grade school.

Wanting to understand family conversation in native languages, I decided to study French as a first year student at Escanaba High School, since studying Croatian was not a curricular option. Though highly motivated to learn a new language, I did not fare well. Actually, I failed miserably and was quite mortified as a result. I vowed never again to study a foreign language.

Ironically, years later, as a third-year student at St. Norbert College, De Pere, WI, I had to study a foreign language or take a foreign literature course to fulfill one of the graduation requirements. Of course I was going to take the Spanish foreign literature course (translated into English). That was my plan of action until Brother Terrence Lauerman, O. Praem., got wind of my "taking the easy way out." Terry challenged me to study Spanish rather than engage in a Spanish literature course; he volunteered to tutor me each weekday evening after dinner. I cautiously agreed. And doing so changed the course of my life and ministry, for which, in retrospect, I am extremely grateful. So you see, in the long run, "failure" can at times be a blessing in disguise, opportunity to new and unforeseen possibilities. And, as I learned, God is at work in experiences of failure, even when we don't realize it.

Yet another gift – that is, a path to healing and homecoming – was given to me by a Hispanic teenager in the company of his parents. This family was a client of mine in my Santa Fe, NM, counseling practice. The young man came to therapy due to poor anger management, as evidenced by disruptive and destructive interactions and behaviors at home, school, and in the community. Therapy was a mix of individual and family sessions that lasted the better part of a year, perhaps somewhat longer. All I know is that our time together seemed interminable because the young man and I were acutely aware that we didn't much like each other. Yet we committed to and engaged in the therapeutic process as best as each of us was able. Mom and dad did the same.

The final day of therapy finally arrived, even though the young man and I thought it never would. There we were, gathered in my office: the teen, his parents, and me. In the last moments of our time together that day, the young man spoke eloquently, and I believe even prophetically: "I know, John, that we don't much like each other, but I have to admit that you helped me and my parents." With mom and dad nodding affirmatively and smiling, the young man continued, "You helped me learn and use anger management skills, and I thank you. Things are better at home, too, as a result of this." Mom and dad again concurred with non-verbal signs of recognition and affirmation. Then came the fateful words from the young man, the mother lode of all gifts, "I don't know if you are Catholic or not, but you would make a good priest. Have you ever thought about it?"

Little did he realize that not only had I thought about it, I was in fact a Roman Catholic priest, though one not in active ministry at the time. Nor did he realize that I had no intention of ever returning to active ministry as a priest. After all, I was doing good and effective "ministry" as a master level clinical Social Worker. What more did I need?

Not only did I leave the office puzzled that day, but truly disturbed, shaken, and unsettled deep within my being. What prophetic message was God speaking to me through this young man and his parents as a result of our therapeutic sojourn? Furthermore, I thought to myself on the drive home, "I have been effective in teaching anger management skills to this family. Now, when might I employ those same skills in my life, family, and friendships? And, moreover, might not this be a call back to the gift of ministerial priesthood?"

Stories of family, friendship, community, and faith - stories of healing and homecoming - are evidence to me of the invitation to trust in God and God's promises throughout history, past, present, and future. They are signs of God's deep and abiding love for me, and for us. In the words of Fr. Nouwen (1996): "...stop running and start trusting and receiving...live out of a new place...the core of your being - your heart...," the place where truth is found and God resides. (pp. 12-14)

I conclude this chapter with a story about my youngest brother, Jim. He was born with significant hearing loss and didn't utter his first words until he was three or four years old. We had developed our own simple sign language over time within the family system which allowed us to communicate well.

After professional evaluations by audiologists, my parents were told that their son would never be able to speak and that he would need to learn sign language. It was also recommended to my parents that they place Jim at the State of Michigan School for the Deaf. Mom was emphatic in her response; Jim would remain at home, he would learn to speak, he would attend school, and she would tutor him. There was no discussion. And no one knows quite how she did it, but mom taught Jim to talk and speak. His ability to use sign language came later.

I recall a family gathering wherein we presented Jim with the idea of getting a Cochlear implant (an electronic medical devise implant near the ear) so that he might hear like the rest of us. We even had some discussion around financially supporting him in this endeavor. His response to us still gives me great pause today. Jim said to us with tears in his eyes: "Did God make a mistake when He created me?" He then continued: "I don't want a Cochlear implant."

Jim taught us to live out of a new place in our hearts, that day, and to hear and receive his truth expressed from the heart, the core of his being . . . the place where truth is found. Fr. Nouwen, and Jim, got it right. Might we get it right, too.

Reflection: Psalm 27

Of what or whom are you afraid?

_____

_____

_____

_____

_____

_____

_____

_____

What does it mean for you "to dwell in the house of the Lord?"

_____

_____

_____

_____

_____

_____

_____

_____

In what ways do you hide your face from the Lord?

_____

_____

_____

_____

_____

_____

_____

_____

_____

What does "waiting for the Lord with courage" mean to you?

_____

_____

_____

_____

_____

_____

_____

_____

In what way(s) is "waiting for the Lord with courage" challenging? In what way(s) is it life-giving?

_____

_____

_____

_____

_____

_____

_____

_____

_____

_____

What "good things of the Lord in the land of the living" do you seek?

_____

_____

_____

_____

_____

_____

_____

Where and how have you failed and/or been humbled in your life? What life-giving and faith-filled lessons have you learned through these experiences?

_____

_____

_____

_____

_____

_____

_____

_____

_____

_____

_____

_____

_____

_____

_____

_____

_____

_____

_____

_____

_____

What experience(s) of "homecoming"- of being welcomed home after a life detour - have you experienced? What life-giving and faith-filled lessons have you learned as a result?

_____

_____

_____

_____

_____

_____

_____

_____

_____

_____

_____

_____

_____

_____

_____

_____

_____

_____

_____

_____

In what ways are you called "to proclaim liberty to captives and recovery of sight to the blind?"

_____

_____

_____

_____

_____

_____

_____

_____

_____

_____

_____

_____

_____

_____

_____

_____

_____

_____

_____

In what ways are you called "to let the oppressed go free, and to proclaim a year acceptable to the Lord?"

_____

_____

_____

_____

_____

_____

_____

_____

_____

_____

_____

_____

_____

_____

_____

_____

_____

_____

_____

_____

CHAPTER TEN
proclaiming hope & Good News

"May the God of hope fill you with all joy and peace in believing, so that
by the power of the Holy Spirit you may abound in hope."
(Romans 15:13)

The reign of God is already here, but not fully. We taste
the joy and know the peace of God's reign among us. Hope
abounds in and through the presence and power of the Holy
Spirit as we anticipate the fullness of the Kingdom. The mission - my work, your work, and our work - remains incomplete.
It is a work in progress. The invitation, of course, continues to

come from the heart - born from the inside out - to reform and live grounded in gospel values. In this way we know that heaven is for real; we that know heaven is for real in ways that we cannot completely see, know, embrace or fully experience on this side of the fullness of eternal life. So, in all humility and Christian charity, and with great hope, we encourage each other to trust and step into living, relating, and loving in new and renewed ways, for doing so is our very participation in the unfathomable mystery of heaven, the reign and kingdom of God at hand.

Always remember the great promise of hope: that, like brother Jesus, the spirit of the Lord is ever upon you. Why? Because "the Lord has anointed you to bring glad tidings to the poor"…that the Lord sends you and sends me - sends us forth - "to proclaim liberty to captives and recovery of sight to the blind, to let the oppressed go free, and to proclaim a year acceptable to the Lord." (Luke 4:18–19)

Proclaiming this very day as the time acceptable to the Lord is a blessing and grace replete with hope - a hope that is essential for the freedom of a life grounded in faith. *The United States Catholic Catechism for Adults* (2006) reminds us: "Hope fills us with the confidence that God accompanies us on our journey through life and guides us to eternal life" (p. 343). Pope Francis (2013) says it this way: "We are on a journey, on a pilgrimage toward the fullness of life, and that fullness of life is what illumines our journey!" Hope lights our way and empowers us to transform the challenges, struggles, uncertainties, and sin of our lives so that we can be fully alive and "share in the glorious freedom of the children of God" (Rm. 8:21b).

The aforementioned teenager, who, during his final counseling session with me and his parents, was an unanticipated disciple and minister of hope when he affirmed my clinical skills and made what seemed to be an innocent observation about what he experienced in his interactions with me as therapist: "John, have you ever thought about being a priest? You would make a good one." Indeed, I would! What he didn't know was that I was a priest...a priest who had lost sight of the promise of hope in my life.

In the days following this fateful encounter, I made a conscious decision to begin addressing the unfinished business of my life. Deciding to take my own best advice to manage differently the unsettled and unresolved disappointment and anger of my life, I placed a phone call to Archbishop Michael Sheehan in Albuquerque to schedule an appointment to meet with him. My intention in doing so was not to request a return to active ministry as a priest but to make amends and apologize for the way I departed from the Archdiocese of Santa Fe...to take ownership of my actions.

Within days I found myself in conversation with the archbishop. He was warm and gracious in his welcome. As I spoke with him, I apologized for the way in which I had informed him of my departure from active priestly ministry some years earlier. There was no dialogue on that day; I simply informed him of my decision to leave active ministry, excused myself from his presence, and was on my way to a new future, or so I thought.

Archbishop Michael listened attentively and graciously accepted my apology. He then invited me to experience the healing balm of the Sacrament of Penance. Together, we prayed for God's continued grace and blessings in my life, as well as for the priests of the Archdiocese of Santa Fe. This prayer of reconciliation and hope was a powerful and transformative moment in our time together, an experience of Christian humility borne of a broken heart and many life struggles. For the first time in a long time, I was at peace.

After thanking the archbishop for his kindnesses to me, I rose from the chair in front of his desk to take leave. As I approached the doorway, he said to me "John, do you ever miss it?" I said "Miss what?," to which he responded "priesthood." I felt tears form in my eyes and run down my cheek. I turned toward him and said "Every day of my life." "Well, then, would you ever come back home, John?" Come home, indeed. While I didn't know what that exactly meant, or what it would entail, "home" is where I so desired to be.

In light of what I experienced as a positive and encouraging reconciliation with the archbishop, I subsequently made a decision to approach the Norbertine Community of New Mexico in anticipation of a similar experience. When I departed from the Norbertine Community some years earlier it was also without much dialogue. I had made up my mind to leave and to incardinate into the Archdiocese of Santa Fe, and that was that. My desire, at least in part, was to serve the needs of Roman Catholics in rural Northern New Mexico where there was a great need for bilingual and culturally sensitive clergy. But, little did I know at the time, I would one day return to the Norbertine Community.

As part of my return to active ministry as a priest of the Archdiocese of Santa Fe, I decided to schedule a private retreat at Norbertine Community Priory of Santa María de la Vid in the South Valley of Albuquerque. After arriving there and making my way to the hermitage assigned to me, I saw that Prior Joel Garner, now abbot, had placed a note on the desk inviting me to take meals with the community. The community was most gracious and hospitable in its welcome, for which I was most grateful, especially in light of some personal anxiety I was experiencing, anxiety that was the result of unfinished business with the Norbertines, or perhaps more accurately stated, with myself.

Dialogue ensued with a community of brothers and continued for several months until one Christmas Eve when we gathered in the community room after dinner to explore the possibility of my returning home to the community. Some days later I recall meeting again with the archbishop to share this unfolding part of my journey, indicating that the Holy Spirit was leading me to return home to the Norbertine Community. He smiled, sat back in his chair, and said: "Who am I to challenge the work of the Holy Spirit? I don't stand a chance." We both laughed.

By God's grace and the support, encouragement, and prayers of many good people, in particular Archbishop Michael, the Norbertine Community, and my Uncle Clem, I had come full circle and was back home. And what a great homecoming it was. I was an active priest and member of the Norbertine Community once again.

An unanticipated part of my homecoming was my request to the Abbot Gary Neville of St. Norbert Abbey, the mother abbey of the New Mexico Norbertine Community, to return to full-time residence and ministry in Wisconsin. My request was due in part to the aging of my dad and stepmom, as well as a desire to be closer to my biological family. It was time to heal and reengage in family and community life back in Wisconsin and Upper Michigan where it all began.

After arriving home at St. Norbert Abbey, my first stop was to visit my Uncle Clem who by this time was residing in the nursing care center at the abbey. He was a seasoned octogenarian, nearly blind, and unable to walk without support. His room was simple: he had his white, Norbertine habit and a few pieces of clothes, several cookbooks - he was a chef by profession - along with a prayer book, crucifix, and rosary on his desk. He also had a small wooden box that contained his gardening tools.

Uncle Clem was seated at his desk praying the rosary as I knocked on his door and greeted him. He instantly recognized my voice, smiled, and extended his arms for a hug, saying: "Welcome home, Johnny. I'm so happy to see you. I have prayed a rosary for you every day since you left. I prayed that God and the Blessed Mother would protect and watch over you. My prayers have been answered and my work is done."

"My work is done," said Uncle Clem. His mission was complete and he knew it. Not long after this graced encounter, he was diagnosed with cancer and entered into the fullness of his eternal reward - heaven, the fullness of the Kingdom of God - on May 3, 2008. It was a privilege for me to preach the homily at the Mass of Christian burial in his honor and memory.

Uncle Clem remains a true gift to me and to many others as well. I know that he continues to love me, pray for me, and watch over me. It is because of him that I remain at home in God – that I remain grounded in matters of the heart – so as to grow into my best self . . . in service of others.

EPILOGUE
faithful companions

"Heaven isn't just a place you go, heaven is how you live your life."
(Meacham, 2012, p. 32)

It's been twenty-two years since my cardiac event. That's a long time. Though the years have passed quickly, my near-death experience continues to be very real and present. I so yearn for the peace of the fullness of heaven for all eternity. In the meantime, as I make my sojourn into the fullness of heaven, I continue to discover the nature and meaning of my mission in the context of Jesus' mission, which, of course, is the mission of all baptized Christians.

Yes, there remain places in my life where I continue to be challenged, places where I am broken and continue to struggle, where I am held captive and remain blinded and oppressed. And, yes, my inner spirit yearns to be set free from these limiting realities and challenges, and, too, from sin itself.

I know that I have made, and continue to make, significant progress in my spiritual journey; however, if I'm going to be honest, there remains interior loneliness from time to time as I make my way. After all of the good ministry and service to and for others, after all the wonderful presentations and talks, and after conducting dynamic, inspiring, and spirit-filled retreats and parish missions, when the end of the day arrives and I close the door of my abbey room, I face the darkness of my humanity, my demons, and my sin much like anyone else. In this I know that I am not alone. This is the irony and mystery of Christian living and loving, of course. Herein, the refreshing words, guidance, and counsel of Fr. Nouwen (1996) on loneliness encourage me and instill hope.

> The spiritual task is not to escape your loneliness,
> not to let yourself drown in it, but to find its
> source…The pain of your loneliness may be root-
> ed in your deepest vocation. You might find that
> your loneliness is linked to your call to live com-

pletely for God. Thus your loneliness may be revealed to you as the other side of your unique gift. Once you can experience in your innermost being the truth of this, you may find your loneliness not only tolerable but even fruitful. What seemed primarily painful may then become a feeling that, though painful, opens for you the way to an even deeper knowledge of God's love. (pp. 36-37)

Loneliness, then, is transformed into pure gift rather than an experience shrouded only in the pain and suffering of the cross. The daily invitation extended to me is to become a man and priest of deep prayer and contemplation, to make my way into the depth of God's love for me.

Healing is not realized independently of significant relationships along life's journey or outside the context of faith. Homecomings of all kinds - intrapersonal, interpersonal, and communal - offer ongoing opportunities for reconciliation and transformation of realities and relationships once thought impossible. This is the "stuff" of the spiritual life, and there is no getting around it or away from it.

As my spiritual journey unfolds - the transformation of my heart - I am simultaneously experiencing a physical transformation, one which has been incredibly affirming and encouraging and, yet, equally challenging and at times somewhat disheartening.

I have struggled throughout my life with being overweight, often reminded by others that I was obese and that I needed to do something about it. Historically, food has been my reward for a job well done; food has been my solace for life's frustrations and disappointments as well.

Some three years ago, I made a difficult and challenging decision to engage in an evaluative medical and psychological process that led to my decision to have gastric sleeve surgery. I've maintained a weight loss of 140 pounds and have a new lease on life. Many have been extremely supportive of me in this transformative process, while others say that they prefer the former "fat" me because I was "more jolly" and didn't have such a strong and decisive voice. Go figure.

This is yet one more example of a lived reality that teaches me about the importance of finding my way home, confidently residing there, and humbly acting with courage, irrespective of what others might say, do, or think about me. For I need not and must not seek the approval of others, but only desire the grace and love of God in Jesus Christ in and through the power and presence of the Holy Spirit.

You keep listening to those who seem to reject you. But they never speak about you. They speak about their own limitations. They confess their poverty in the face of your needs and desires. They simply ask for your compassion. They do not say that you are bad, ugly, or despicable. They say only that you are asking for something they cannot give and that they need to get some distance from you to survive emotionally. The sadness is that you perceive their necessary withdrawal as a rejection of you instead of as a call to return home and discover there your true belovedness. (Nouwen, 2001 p. 13)

I am "beloved" and I am at "home." And I pray each and every day that I never lose sight of being loved. I pray as well that I may not wander too far from the home of my heart where the fullness and love of God reside in abundance.

Finally, I come to understand, believe, and live the poetic words my mother left me in the form of a card shortly before her death in 1989. The poem by Susan Polis Schultz reads:

To see you happy – laughing and joking, smiling and content, striving towards the goals of your own, accomplishing what you set out to do, having fun with yourself and your friends, capable of loving and being loved – is what I always wished for you. Today I thought about your handsome face and felt your excitement for life and your genuine happiness and I, as your mother burst with pride as I realized that my dreams for you came true. What an extraordinary person you have become; and, as you continue to grow, please remember always how very much I love you.

Mom signed the card "and God bless you. Love and prayers, Mom." Indeed, God blesses; and, for sure, love survives death.

The seeds of death are at work in us, but love is stronger than death. Your death and mine is our final passage, our exodus to the full realization of our identity as God's beloved children and to full communion with the God of love. Jesus walked the path ahead of us and invites us to choose the same faith during our lifetime. He calls to us, "Follow me." He assures us, "Do not be afraid." This is our faith. (Nouwen, 2001, pp. 154 – 155)

I have come full circle and I choose to conclude, at least for now, where I began: a dedication in memory of my mother, Elizabeth Tourangeau, and my friend, Cari Schartner. They remain two important women in my life because they taught and continue to teach me how to follow Jesus, how to be free and no longer afraid, and how to trust God before all else.

The book ends here, but the pilgrimage – the journey – continues.

Amen.

Reflection: Loneliness as faithful companion on the journey

What do you think about Fr. Nouwen's statement that "the pain of your loneliness may be rooted in your deepest vocation?"

_____

_____

_____

_____

_____

_____

_____

_____

_____

_____

_____

_____

_____

_____

_____

_____

_____

Through the loneliness and pain of your life, how are you being called to "live completely for God?"

_____

_____

_____

_____

_____

_____

_____

_____

_____

_____

_____

_____

_____

_____

_____

_____

_____

In what way(s) could your loneliness be "gift" and bear fruit in your life and for others?

_____

_____

_____

_____

_____

_____

_____

_____

_____

_____

_____

_____

_____

_____

_____

_____

_____

_____

_____

In what way(s) does your loneliness dispose you for yet "deeper knowledge of God's love" for you?

_____

_____

_____

_____

_____

_____

_____

_____

_____

_____

_____

_____

_____

_____

_____

_____

_____

_____

_____

_____

Reflection: Developing a
Personal Mission Statement

The personal mission of Jesus, a mission given to all of us in and through the Sacrament of Baptism and grounded in the ancient vision of the prophet Isaiah (see Luke 4:18b-19), can be summed up in one sentence: "The Son of Man has come to search out and save what was lost." (Luke 19:10)

We, like Jesus, are called to "search out and save what is lost" in our personal lives, in our families and churches, and in the world at large. But in order to do so and be effective, it's important for each of us to consider our mission in Jesus Christ. With the articulation of a living and personal mission statement, we stake our claim by identifying our beliefs, core values, and goals; that is what we will focus on and carry forth in faith and what we will and must leave behind.

The articulation of a personal mission statement does not happen overnight. It is the fruit of a long and often arduous spiritual process over time. A statement of personal mission is a living reality that grows and changes with us and through our relationship with God.

What follows are some helpful "hints" (in the form of questions) for the articulation of a personal mission statement, many of which have been reflected upon in this companion workbook and journal. Remember that an effective mission statement of any kind must be measurable; that is, a way of letting yourself and others know that you are succeeding and accomplishing the mission you intend.

What are your favorite stories from Sacred Scripture and who are the main characters therein?

If asked, what would your family and friends say your strengths are? Conversely, where is growth/change/improvement still needed?

_____

_____

_____

_____

_____

_____

_____

_____

_____

_____

_____

_____

_____

_____

_____

_____

_____

_____

How do you want to make a difference in your family, community, and the world as a person of faith?

_____

_____

_____

_____

_____

_____

_____

_____

_____

_____

_____

_____

_____

_____

_____

_____

_____

_____

What must you leave behind to welcome and embrace a renewed sense of mission to others in the name of Jesus?

_____

_____

_____

_____

_____

_____

_____

_____

_____

_____

_____

_____

_____

_____

_____

_____

_____

_____

_____

What are my core beliefs (i.e., personal, familial, communal, etc.) and values?

What do I want the purpose of my life to be?

_____

_____

_____

_____

_____

_____

_____

_____

_____

_____

_____

_____

_____

_____

_____

_____

_____

_____

_____

Scriptural context for reflection and journaling:

"Moses said to the people: 'Hear, O Israel! The Lord is our God, the Lord alone! Therefore, you shall love the Lord, your God, with all your heart, and with all your soul, and with all your strength. Take to heart these words which I enjoin on you today. Drill them into your children. Speak of them at home and abroad, whether you are busy or at rest. Bind them at your wrist as a sign and let them be as a pendant of our forehead. Write them on the doorposts of your houses and on your gates.
(Deuteronomy 6:5-9)

ARTICULATION OF PERSONAL MISSION STATEMENT:

_____

_____

_____

_____

_____

_____

_____

_____

_____

_____

_____

_____

Reflection: Personal Prayer & Mission

"Gracious and loving God,

As I begin this new day, help me to appreciate the importance of living in the here-and-now, not hoping for tomorrow or worrying about yesterday.

Expect me to be a son who honors his parents, a brother who sets the example, a husband who adores his wife, a father who cherishes his children, and a man who seeks to do your will.

Support my efforts to be an instrument of your peace, a friend to the lonely, a host to the poor, and a voice for those whose words have fallen on deaf ears.

Challenge me to live a life whereby others might be able to recognize your goodness in me, just as I am able to find you in them.

Grant me the courage to proclaim proudly and boldly my faith to any person, in any place, at any time.

Keep me forever in your living care and continue to be my guiding light on my journey back to you.

I pray this in your name. Amen.

Mother Mary, pray for me."

Personal Prayer and Mission of Travis J. Vanden Heuvel

What is your prayer to God *today*?

How can you be more effective in "living in the here-and-now?"

_____

_____

_____

_____

_____

_____

_____

_____

_____

_____

_____

_____

_____

_____

_____

_____

_____

_____

_____

_____

In what ways might you be more loving and compassionate?

Is "family" the centerpiece of your life? Why or why not?

_____

_____

_____

_____

_____

_____

_____

_____

_____

_____

_____

_____

_____

_____

_____

_____

_____

_____

Life is about others. What efforts are you making to be an instrument of God's peace, justice, and mercy to others?

_____

_____

_____

_____

_____

_____

_____

_____

_____

_____

_____

_____

_____

_____

_____

_____

_____

_____

In what ways do you need to be challenged in your Christian life? Are you willing to be challenged?

_____

_____

_____

_____

_____

_____

_____

_____

_____

_____

_____

_____

_____

_____

_____

_____

_____

_____

_____

APPENDIX
born into the fullness of eternal life

"Indeed for your faithful, Lord, life is changed not ended, and,
when this earthly dwelling turns to dust, an eternal dwelling
is made ready for them in heaven."
(Preface of Christian Death I, 2011, p. 622)

For the reader who may be interested, I'm including the homilies I preached at the Masses of Christian Burial for my mother and Cari Schartner; both remain influential women in my life.

Elizabeth Ann (Kutches) Tourangeau

1936 – 1989

Wisdom 4:7-11, 13-15

Psalm 27

II Corinthians 4:7-15

Luke 2:15-20

God must have been very lonely on Monday. That's why I suspect God decided to visit our home on the Gross Hill. When God came to us that evening, God held each of us very closely…God pondered the marvelous creation at work in each of us…taking great delight in the goodness of it all. Then, in what seemed to be an instant, God decided to take from our midst the one who was the loveliest of all…the most beautiful, the most holy, the most loving, the most tender…the one we call "mom"…the one dad calls "dear"…the one you fondly call "sis"…or "Liz," your dear friend…your "auntie"…and to Jeremy, Danny, Roger III and little Sara Elizabeth, the one you call "grandma"…the special person in your life who loved you as only a grandma could.

My dear mother was a shy, quiet, humble, and retreating kind of person. She was also a very passionate woman…a woman of great conviction. Mom's three greatest passions in this life were her love of God, her children/grandchildren, and her husband.

First of all, in order to grasp mom's love of God, we need to focus our attention on the central symbol of our Christian faith: the CROSS of Jesus Christ. Our second reading speaks of this mystery in a powerful way. St. Paul wrote:

> We are afflicted in every way possible, but we are not crushed; full of doubts, we never despair. We are persecuted but never abandoned; we are struck down but never destroyed. Continually we carry about in our bodies the dying of Jesus, so that in our bodies the life of Jesus may also be revealed.

Mom carried many crosses in this life...and she did so with great courage and without fanfare. In weakness she was made strong. Mom's example of carrying the cross of Jesus makes each of us strong in our own weakness. Mom's passion for full union with the "God of all strength" is her number one gift to us.

Secondly, mom was passionate with respect to her kids...me, Roger Jr., Kathy, and Jimmy...and, of course, our sister Kristine whom we never knew, but one mom often called her little angel of God watching over us from the heavens. Like Mary in the Gospel story today, mom "treasured and pondered in her heart" the mystery of God at work in each of us.

In all honesty, mom gifted me by nurturing my priestly vocation as only a loving mother could do...a loving mother who always introduced me to her friends by saying: "Please meet my son John, the priest." I am so very proud and honored to be her son and especially today to be "her priest!"

Mom's love of family life is clearly present in Roger and Kathy. Rog and Sis, your tender, gentle, and loving interaction with your spouses and children is really mom's dream come true for each of you. She was and is so proud of the family life you share.

Mom has given an extra-special gift to Jimmy...the gift of teaching. Clearly, mom gave you, Jimmy, the gift of speech...hours and hours and hours of endless teaching that have taught you to talk...a gift that has opened so very many doors for you, a great gift that has allowed you to go out into the world touching and healing the lives of many people, not only in the deaf world, but also in the hearing world.

May mom's selfless love, generous spirit, and genuine concern for others always be at work in us, her dear children.

Thirdly, mom was passionate with respect to her husband, our dad, whose hand she took in marriage before the altar of God some thirty-three years ago. In her pain and suffering, mom could still tell dad how much she loved him. She could weep in his arms and ask "Why?" She could still look him straight in the eye, smile ever so lovingly, and with a twinkle in her eyes, share the depth of her heart with him. Mom's faithfulness and fidelity are her passionate and loving gifts to the man she loved. It is true, then, what the Book of Wisdom says of life in the first reading:

> Length of days is not what makes age honorable,
> nor number of years the true measure of life...for
> grace and mercy await the chosen of the Lord,
> and protection to the Lord's holy ones.

Dad, may you always cherish the great gifts mom gave you.

Mom's concern was always for us, her family, and loved ones. She makes us strong by walking with us in our weakness. Even in her painful fight with cancer, mom was a great source of strength to all around her. Because of her many gifts - because of the very person that she was in this life - she has been purified and made one of God's holy Saints in heaven...sitting at the great Banquet Table with Kristine Ann, her parents (grandpa and grandma Kutches), brothers Jim and Frank, and her sisters Bede (Ann) and Onie (Leona).

Mom's spirit continues to be present to us in a powerful way. Cancer may have taken her life, but it did not touch her spirit! Her spirit lives on in each of us, even in the newest member of our family: Sara Elizabeth, her namesake, born only a few months ago. From death comes new life... new life for mom and for us here on earth.

We give thanks for the gift of mom - for the gift of her whole life - as we now gather around the Table of the Lord...a holy Table from which mom was spiritually fed and nourished for many years. We break bread...we share the one cup...gifts that nourish each of us for our journey to fuller life with God and all the Saints.

Mom's passing from this life to the next has left our hearts broken. Yet, in the mystery of it all, I understand a bit better why God decided to visit the Tourangeau home on the Gross Hill this past Monday evening...calling the one who was the most faithful, the loveliest, holiest, and purest of all to the newness of life everlasting!

Cari Lynn (Colombo) Schartner

1957 – 2014

Isaiah 25: 6a, 7-9

II Corinthians 4:14-5:1

Luke 23:44-46, 50, 52-53; 24:1-6a

Tia and Paul, to you and your children, and to you Frankie and Lindsey on the death of "mom," and to Dena, Cheri, and Bart on the death of your "sister," and to you who are members of Cari's extended family and circle of friendship, please receive our deepest sympathy at this time of significant loss. Know that you do not journey alone; we are family of blood and family of faith, both of which were and continue to be central in Cari's life...in her marriage to Frank, with her children and family, in her work—her ministry—as financial expert/bookkeeper/manager at Prince of Peace Catholic Church, for the GRACE (Green Bay Area Catholic Education, Inc.) system, and St. Norbert College Parish.

Tia and Frankie, I was struck by what you wrote in your mom's obituary: "Our mother's Christ-centered faith was very important to her. Her infectious energy could put a smile on anyone near her. Family meant everything to Cari." And, she was so proud to be grandma to Will and Zita, her pride and joy.

Cari was educated here at Saints Peter and Paul (Institute, WI) under the guidance of the Franciscan Sisters of the Holy Cross (Bay Settlement Sisters). Education and learning were very important to her. I suspect that's why she was so very proud of the college education that both Tia and Frankie completed. What a proud and grateful mother she was.

On another note, Cari so deeply desired to be part of Frankie and Lindsey's April wedding. The marriage did take place this past Wednesday at Tia and Paul's home with Fr. Patrick presiding. Cari was filled with joy...and...she will be present in April with you, but in a different/more profound way! "For in death, life is changed, not ended. When the body of our early dwelling lies in death, we gain an everlasting dwelling place in heaven."

And what is heaven? One author suggests: "Heaven isn't just a place you go. Heaven is how you live your life." And the Gospel writer Luke (17:21b) says: "The reign of God is already in your midst." The Gospel writer Mark (1:15) says it this way: "This is the time of fulfillment. The reign of God is at hand!" Yes, indeed, heaven is already present in our midst and this is the time of heaven's fulfillment! That's why we are encouraged to repent and believe...to embrace gospel mission, gospel living, and gospel loving.

Trappist monk, priest, and mystic, Thomas Merton says this about heaven:

"Heaven is love...God is a consuming fire. If we, by love become transformed into God and burn as God burns, God's fire will be our everlasting joy...When we love God we find joy in all things. We are one with God and others."

Moreover, John Paul II at a general audience in 1999 said: "Heaven is neither an abstraction nor a physical place in the clouds, but a living, personal relationship with the Holy Trinity," with the fullness of God and in the company of all the saints. Finally, *The Catechism of the Catholic Church* teaches us: "Heaven is complete intimacy with God as a result of our participation in Christ's paschal mystery;" that is, in the living, suffering, dying, and rising to new life.

And, so, as we enter more deeply into Christ's paschal mystery, we find strength and encouragement in the readings we heard a short time ago.

From the Second letter of Paul to the Corinthians: We know that the one who raised the Lord Jesus will raise us also...Therefore, we are not discouraged; rather, although our outer self is wasting away, our inner self is being renewed day by day...For we know that if your earthly dwelling, a tent, should be destroyed, we have a building from God, a dwelling not made with hands, eternal in heaven.

From the Gospel of St. Luke, Jesus utters: "Father, into your hands I commend my spirit." Cari prayed for this same grace to hand over her spirit, saying to me a few days ago: "I hope I can accept death with humility when the time comes." And, in the next breath she said: "Fr. John, is there anything I can do for you?" "Yes," I replied. "When you get to heaven greet my mom for me. You'll know who she is, don't worry."

We embrace the hope given us by the angels in dazzling garments in Luke's gospel story: "Do not seek the living one among the dead. He is not here." Jesus lives! And, so, too, Cari lives! She is not here; she has been raised.

The Prophet Isaiah assures us that "...the Lord of hosts provides for all peoples ... the Lord destroys death forever ... This is the Lord for whom we looked; let us rejoice and be glad that we are saved!"

Rejoicing is what Cari desired; and, it is what she asks of us today. "I don't want any crying at my funeral ... no "On Eagles Wings" song because it makes everyone cry. I want a celebration ... be thankful for the time we had."

And celebrate we do, Cari … Rest in peace holy child of God! Know that I am/we are most grateful for your faith-filled spirit, encouragement, and friendship on the Journey … a Journey that continues for all eternity.

REFERENCES

Albom, M. (2003). *The Five People You Meet in Heaven*. New York: Hyperion.

Barry, P. M., Taylor, M., & Torch, S. (2014). *Song for the Lonely*. (http://artists.letssingit.com/cher-lyrics-song-for-the-lonely-22d5wd2#axzz3Xh9v6wqN)

Burpo, T., & Vincent, L. (2010). *Heaven is for Real: A Little Boy's Astounding Story of his Trip to Heaven*. Nashville: Thomas Nelson, Inc.

Catherine of Siena. (1980). *Catherine of Siena: The Dialogue*. New York: Paulist Press.

Catholic Church & Vatican Council II (2nd: 1962 – 1965). (1983). *Sacramentary: The Roman Missal revised by the decree of the Second Vatican Ecumenical Council and published by authority of Pope Paul VI.* Ottawa: Publications Service, CCCB.

Catholic Church. (2012). *Catechism of the Catholic Church* (2nd ed.). Vatican City: Libreria Editrice Vaticana.

Higginson, T. W. (1897). *The procession of the flowers and kindred papers.* New York: Longmans, Green, and Co.

Keller, T. (2008). *The Reason for God: Belief in an Age of Skepticism.* New York: Penguin Group, Inc.

Meacham, J. (2012, April 16). *Heaven can't wait: Why rethinking the hereafter could make the world a better place.* Time, 30 – 36.

Merton, T. (1948). *Seeds of contemplation.* Norfolk: James Laughlin.

Nouwen, H. (1972). *The Wounded Healer: Ministry in Contemporary Society.* New York: Image Doubleday.

Nouwen, H. (1996). *The Inner Voice of Love: A Journey Through Anguish to Freedom.* New York: Doubleday.

Nouwen, H. (2001). *Finding My Way Home.* New York: The Cross road Publishing Company.

Piper, D., & Murphey, C. (2004). *90 Minutes in Heaven: A True Story of Death and Life.* Grand Rapids: Revell.

Pope Benedict XVI.Spe Salvi. Retrieved on April 28, 2015, from

http://w2.vatican.va/content/benedictxvi/en/encyclicals/docu
ments/hf_ben-xvi_enc_20071130_spe-salvi.html

Pope Francis. (2013). Angelus. Retrieved on April 29, 2015, from
https://w2.vatican.va/content/francesco/en/angelus/2013/docu
ments/papa-francesco_angelus_20131110.html

Pope John Paul II. (1999). *Heaven, Hell and Purgatory*. Retrieved
on September 1, 2013 from https://www.ewtn.com/library/
PAPALDOC/JP2HEAVEN.HTM

Preface of Christian Death I, in *The Roman Missal*, trans. The Inter-
national Commission on English in the Liturgy, 3rd typical
ed., Washington D.C.: Unites States Catholic Conference of
Bishops, 2011.

Shannon, W. H. (1998). A note to the reader. *The Seven Storey
Mountain* (First Harvest Edition ed., pp. xix-xxiii). New
York: Harcourt, Inc.

USCCB. (2006). *The United States Catholic Catechism for Adults*.
Washington, D.C.: United States Catholic Conference of
Bishops.

Williamson, M. (1992). *A return to love: Reflections on the principles of a course in miracles*. New York: Harper Collins.

Rev. John M. Tourangeau, O. Praem.
Travis J. Vanden Heuvel

Co-founders | *Peregrino Press*
Co-authors | *To Heaven & Back: The Journey of a Roman Catholic Priest*

Peregrino Press (that is, "Pilgrim" Press translated from Spanish to English) is a media publishing company in De Pere, WI. Born out of a desire to share our stories and our faith more intimately, Peregrino Press publishes engaging and inspired content that enhances and promotes our Catholic identity.

As children of God – and as brothers and sisters in Christ – we all journey together. The image of being on a pilgrimage finds meaning in walking with others on life's journey, for no one of us is meant to "go-it-alone." Simply, in Christ, we are pilgrims and friends on a profound journey of faith. And it is in the sharing of the stories of our lives that we come to new life, hope, and peace.

More about Fr. John

John has been an ordained priest for nearly 30 years and is a member of the Norbertine Community residing at St. Norbert Abbey in De Pere, WI.

Since 2012, John has been traveling around the country sharing his life story in a presentation titled "Heaven: Is it for real?" From 2012 to 2015, more than 10,000 people attended more than 35 presentations. The success with which these presentations were received has resulted in the publishing of *To Heaven & Back: The Journey of a Roman Catholic Priest* by John Tourangeau and Travis Vanden Heuvel.

A thumbnail sketch of John's life as a Norbertine and priest includes service as a transitional deacon and newly ordained priest at Providence of God Parish (Chicago, IL), followed by a move to the Archdiocese of Santa Fe, NM. There he served as Parochial Vicar at Our Lady of the Most Holy Rosary Catholic Community (Albuquerque, NM), followed by pastorates at St. Gertrude Parish (Mora, NM), Our Lady of Guadalupe Parish (Clovis, NM), San Francisco de Asís Parish (Ranchos de Taos, NM), and St. Anne Parish (Albuquerque, NM). During those years John also served as Vicar Forane (Dean) and later as a member of the Presbyteral Council. Later, John would return to St. Norbert Abbey and serve as Vocation Coordinator and Pastor of St. Norbert College Parish.

John did his undergraduate studies at St. Norbert College in De Pere, WI. He holds a Master of Divinity Degree with Mission Specialization from Catholic Theological Union (CTU) in Chicago (1986), a Master of Social Work Degree (MSW) from New Mexico Highlands University, Las Vegas, NM (1997). He is currently a Licensed Clinical Social Worker (LCSW) in the State of Wisconsin.

John also holds a Master of Business Administration Degree (MBA) from The University of Phoenix, Albuquerque, NM (2003), and is in the dissertation phase of a Ph.D. in Organization Development.

CPSIA information can be obtained
at www.ICGtesting.com
Printed in the USA
LVOW10s1626240517
535701LV00017B/907/P